THE
RECORD HOUSES
COLLECTION IV

1993 1994 1995

Compiled from
Architectural Record,
April 1993 (Vol. 181, No. 4)
April 1994 (Vol. 182, No. 4)
April 1995 (Vol. 183, No. 4)
Copyright 1993, 1994, 1995 by The McGraw-Hill Companies, Inc.

Cover:
T- House, Wilton, New York
Simon Ungers and Tom Kinslow, Architects
© Eduard Hueber photo

Contents 1993

Note of Explanation:
This book consists of pages printed at the same time the actual magazines were printed. As a result of this, the page numbers for each year are those from the original issue.

1993

As Frank Lloyd Wright said in one of his 1930 Kahn Lectures at Princeton University: "Human houses should not be like boxes, blazing in the sun, nor should we outrage the machine by trying to make dwelling-places too complementary to machinery. Any building for humane purposes should be an elemental, sympathetic feature of the ground, complementary to its nature-environment, belonging by kinship to the terrain. A house is not going anywhere, if we can help it." Some of the houses featured in the 38th annual RECORD HOUSES issue are closer than others to Wright's ideal and thereby reflect a refreshing lack of reigning style. Each house is a portrait of the owner and the architect. Collectively, the houses tell the story of architecture in the 1990s, shaped as it is by evolving ideas of family, limited financial resources, and newly pressing environmental concerns. For Stanley Tigerman (page 72), Frank Israel (page 100), and San Francisco firm Tanner Leddy Maytum Stacy (page 84), who have produced larger-scale works in the past, a residential commission is an opportunity to reassess the state of their own art. For principals of younger firms like partners Deborah Berke and Carey McWhorter (page 90) and Gisue and Mojgan Hariri (page 76), a full-fledged house can be a breakthrough. For firms like Bentley LaRosa Salasky (page 94) and William Bruder (page 64), who built their reputations on residential design, each new project is a chance to enrich their study of this most elemental building type. *K. D. S.*

Manufacturers' Sources listed on page 119

Desert Shield

For a retired couple and their animals, Will Bruder designed a house that captures desert views in every room.

*Theuer Residence
Phoenix, Arizona
William P. Bruder, Architect*

Desert buildings are about sun and walls," states architect Will Bruder, who left his native Wisconsin for Phoenix in the early 1970s. An apprenticeship with Paolo Soleri and a lifetime appreciation of Frank Lloyd Wright have left Bruder with a keen eye for tying architecture to the landscape. For Robert Theuer, a retired airline pilot, and his wife Rhonda, Bruder designed a 2,500-square-foot house that embraces the rugged land in a sweeping curve. On one side of that curve is a desert garden, stocked with more than 40 species of local plants, while on the other lies a suburban wasteland of expensive tract homes. Relying on a simple palette of cinderblock, glass, weathered steel, and copper, Bruder erected solid walls facing the subdivision and glass ones looking north to the garden and the South Mountains in the distance.

Like traditional Southwestern houses, this one turns a weather-toughened face to the street and provides a sheltered forecourt only to those who have been allowed past the front gate. Although this inward-looking elevation contrasts with the more expansive north facade, it introduces many of the elements that give the house its character: bold curves, maintenance-free materials, and indigenous landscaping. Peeling away a concrete-block wall from the main house to form the forecourt, Bruder makes it clear from the start that this is an architecture of walls set in motion by the sun. And by hinting at what's to come, the architect has added a sense of mystery to the house's allure.

From the forecourt, the house reveals itself slowly. A recessed entry, designed as an elegant composition of glass planes set between a polished-concrete floor and a particle-board ceiling, draws the visitor indoors. Once inside, subtlety gives way to the spectacular view of the garden and the mountains beyond. Centered on a point 50 feet into the garden, the curving geometry of the north wall draws the eye to the outdoors. Ten-foot-high panels of half-inch-thick glass rise the full height of the wall, offering uninterrupted views.

"We wanted the outside in and the inside out," says Robert Theuer, "and Will certainly did a number on that." One example is a stainless-steel fireplace that sits half inside and half outside the glazed wall. Resting on a seven-foot-wide circular pan of water, the gas fireplace seems to hover between contrasting worlds.

Instead of having separate living, dining, and family rooms, the house has one great room that provides the free-flowing living space the clients had requested. Even the kitchen works as an extension of the living area, separated by only a slender cantilevered counter. The sense of spaciousness is heightened by the contrast between the 10-foot-tall, glazed wall on the north and the seven-and-a-half-foot-high masonry wall on the south. Adding a final touch of drama to the composition is a one-inch-high strip of clerestory window sandwiched between the cinderblock wall and the low ceiling.

The single-loaded-corridor plan ensures that all rooms face the garden and provides cross ventilation to help cool the house. Roof overhangs also protect the house from the sun—three feet beyond the solid south wall and five feet beyond the glazed north wall. Further sun protection comes from a series of perforated-weathered-steel shade "sails" that hang from the roof above the covered garden terrace. A covered stable just west of the house and a dog run adjacent to the guest wing accommodate the clients' two horses and two Great Danes. Both for humans and animals, the house encourages what Bruder calls "resort living," a term that implies spending as much time outdoors as indoors. *Clifford A. Pearson*

Built on a one-acre lot in a suburban subdivision, the Theuer Residence faces its neighbors with a set of curving masonry walls that only hint at what's inside (opposite top). A concrete-block wall with some blocks rotated so they create a perforated effect encloses an outdoor forecourt. The entry gate to the forecourt is made of punched weathered-steel (opposite bottom left), as are the curving shade "sails" protecting the garden terrace on the opposite side of the house (above). The recessed entry is a play of rough and smooth materials (opposite below right). The structural system combines wood framing, load-bearing masonry walls, and steel members along the glazed north wall (previous pages and top).

Heart of the house is a great curving room that includes living and dining areas, as well as a kitchen (previous pages). A particle-board ceiling with maple battens slopes up to meet the 10-foot-high butt-glazed wall overlooking the garden. Bruder relied on a simple palette of materials such as maple-plywood paneling and cinderblock for walls and polished concrete for floors. A snaking line of quarter-inch-thick stainless steel and "bush-hammered" concrete picks up the curving motif found in much of the house (previous pages).

A stainless-steel fireplace, set half indoors and half outdoors, features a gas flame that seems to float on a seven-foot-wide pan of water (opposite). The water runs down a 50-foot-long trough slicing through the garden, then is recycled. The garden is planted with over 40 species of native plants and requires little watering. Because the house looks onto a nature preserve, even the master bedroom (bottom left) and master bath (top left) enjoy floor-to-ceiling glazing. A three-zone heat-pump system provides heating and air-conditioning.

Credits
*Theuer Residence
Phoenix, Arizona*
Owners: *Rhonda and Robert Theuer*
Architect: *William P. Bruder, Architect—William Bruder, principal-in-charge; Wendell Burnette, Robert Adams, Tyler Green, design team*
Engineers: *Jack Trummer, JT Engineering (structural); Roy Otterbein (mechanical/ plumbing)*
Consultants: *Roger Smith, Lighting Dynamics (lighting); Randy Hall, Ray Electric (electrical)*
Landscape Architect: *Christy Ten Eyck, The Planning Center*
General Contractor: *Owner/builder*

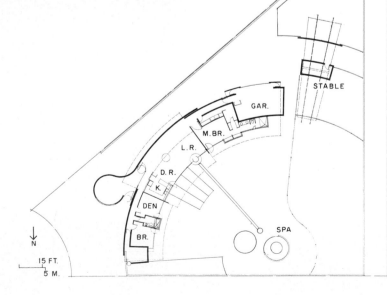

Beachfront Basilica

Stanley Tigerman melds Midwestern barn imagery and traditional church planning to create a winter home/studio for a Chicago-based artist.

Artist's Studio and Residence
La Conchita, California
Tigerman McCurry, Architect

"His work depicts American life, not necessarily in a celebratory fashion but rather by exaggeration, presenting it in a way that enhances the uncertainty we have about it." Stanley Tigerman could be talking about himself—"a bit of autobiography creeps into all of my architecture," he admits—but in fact he is describing the paintings of Chicago-based artist Roger Brown, Tigerman's client for a 1,500-square-foot studio and winter home in La Conchita, California.

Tigerman also looked for inspiration to his own vacation house in Michigan, done in collaboration with partner and wife Margaret McCurry in 1983. Tigerman freely combined his own architectural history with established building types and construction methods to show, in his words, "how disgruntled I am with traditional architecture." His proposed alternative, a pink-stuccoed gambrel-roofed loft-house, is a new hybrid—one that, at first glance, seems out of place in its neighborhood of ramshackle beachfront bungalows.

Tigerman and Brown consider the studio a basilica; the neighbors call it a barn. As Tigerman points out, both structures provide similar amenities: large open space and generous natural light, which were prerequisites for Brown's paintings. Here the "side aisles" are used as a changing gallery for work in progress. A galley kitchen and bathroom core separate a small living area from a spartan bedroom; additional rooms were precluded by the small size of the septic tank, the only size permitted on a clay soil lot. Rolling garage doors close off the living area from the studio and both are aired by natural cross ventilation and giant ceiling-mounted fans. Instead of an altar terminating the space, windows and glass doors in the south wall provide sweeping views of the Pacific Ocean across nearby fields and a freeway.

Outside, Tigerman has attempted to integrate the exterior with its surroundings, what Brown jokingly refers to as "a hippy-dippy community" located 15 miles south of Santa Barbara, by planting a row of palm trees out front and finishing the wood-framed structure in a pink stucco intended to match the color of a nearby Mission church. There is a playfully surreal quality to the overall grouping of house, carport, and garage, heightened by the contrast of a galvanized metal roof and off-the-shelf doors, windows, and hardware—the combination is a gentle reminder of the "magic realism" of Brown's, and his architect's, work. *Aaron Betsky*

Ready-made wood trusses cross the 30-by 50-foot loftlike space at regular intervals. A "view altar" oriented toward the Pacific Ocean is topped by one of Brown's crucifix paintings. The exterior color and the seismic tension rods connecting interior trusses offer clues to the house's California location.

Credits
Artist's Studio and Residence
La Conchita, California
Owner: *Roger Brown*
Architect: *Tigerman McCurry—Stanley Tigerman, Tom McKercher, project team*
Engineers: *D. B. S. Structural Engineering (structural); Al Nibecker & Associates, Inc. (mechanical); Tierra Tech Testing Lab, Inc. (soil/concrete)*
General Contractor: *Phoenix Construction Co.*

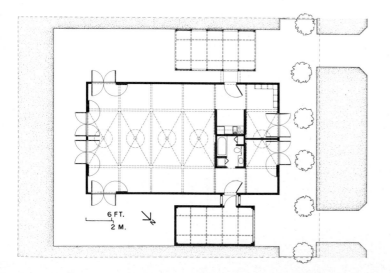

6 FT.
2 M.

Sum of Its Parts

Gorman Residence
New Canaan, Connecticut
Hariri & Hariri Design, Architects

Although made of different pieces—old and new, gable-roofed and barrel-vaulted—the Gorman Residence is greater than the sum of its parts. Faced with an early 1900s carriage house and the changes made to it over the years, architects Gisue and Mojgan Hariri added several major new pieces of their own design, making everything snap into place like a good jigsaw puzzle. While all the elements retain their identities, they fit together—visually and structurally—so that removal of one would imperil the whole.

The project began with Donna and Geoffrey Gorman asking the Hariri sisters to add a second story to a freestanding garage and connect it to the 1,500-square-foot house. The architects also agreed to reconfigure circulation in the house, so the front door wouldn't lead directly into the living room. As the clients began planning for a family, the program grew. In the end, the Hariris recommended tearing down the garage, and building on its foundations a new two-story structure with a family room/den on the ground floor and bedrooms above. In the process, the garage would be pushed farther west and a new entry component would be inserted between the old house and the new family-room structure.

In designing the new elements, the architects kept in mind traditional New England building types. Thus, the family-room building became a "barn" with a barrel-vaulted roof and the connecting element became a "covered bridge" made of glass and steel. Built as a hybrid structure combining wood framing with some steel columns and beams, the new components overlap and penetrate each other so that part of the fun of walking through the house is marveling at how the pieces come together. A good place to appreciate this is inside the curving entrance hall (following pages) where a winding staircase on the south end leads to the second-story bridge and a set of three steps at the other end provides access to the family room. A column near the family room marks the southeast corner of the old garage foundations and helps support the new bridge, thereby serving as both a figurative and literal link between past and present.

Uncomfortable with the ad-hoc nature of the existing house, the clients asked the Hariris to create more free-flowing spaces. Their response was to open the living room directly onto what had been an enclosed porch and what now serves as the dining room. Also added was a new glazed entrance at the south end of the living room that leads onto a generous terrace. "Simple surfaces and straight-forward design give our work a machine-like quality," says Gisue Hariri, recognizing her debt to early Modern architects. "But we like to think that our use of space and our search for connections give it a spirituality and a concern with human psychology that were sometimes missing in early Modernism." *Clifford A. Pearson*

New components double the size of the house to 3,000 square feet. Old and new elements are finished with gray stucco, but each retains its own form and identity (opposite top). Connecting the old house with the additions are a second-story bridge (opposite bottom right) and a terrace on top of the new garage (opposite bottom left).

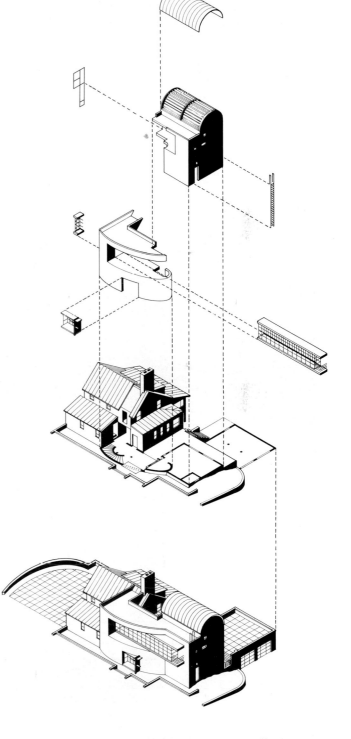

© John Hall photos

Martin Residence
Kennett Square, Pennsylvania
Tanner Leddy Maytum Stacy
Architects

Box Inside Box

The Martin house, situated in conservative Chester County, Pennsylvania, farm country, is a curious study in contrasts—a working couple returning East from San Francisco, he a molecular biologist, she an abstract painter, enlisted an architect known for free-flowing California-style high-tech (see RECORD HOUSES, April 1992, page 124) to design a house in a region known for 19th-century farm complexes with walls of 20-inch thick stone and hand-hewn oak tree trunks for beams.

If ever there was a case of eating your cake and having it too, this house is it. Respecting the 10-acre site of rolling land and the unwritten but powerful local dictates controling the facades of new buildings, the architects wanted to meet the owners' program of accommodating two careers, entertainment of large groups but with all affairs catered (no need for a huge country kitchen). So they simply inserted a new box inside an existing one (see drawing at right). (Of the various buildings on their site, the owners decided to make their home in the barn, restore the carriage house into a guest house, make the corncrib into a garage, add a new building up the hill for a painter's studio, and not purchase the farm house at all.) The new box, faced with cherrywood, is a self-contained structure, imposing no loads upon the rough stone shell. The three-foot perimeter space between the two boxes accommodates circulation, fireplaces, and intimate seating areas close to the light. The inner box carries all structural loads, either on a series of square steel tubes or wide flange posts (depending on the floor), with built-up steel beams, as well as wiring, heating, and plumbing distribution.

The only modifications to the stone shell occur at the entry, a steel-plated box that penetrates the stone envelope; on the opposite side, where a large veranda leads off the main living area; and the enlargement of what is known in those parts as "wind eyes"—small rectangular unglazed holes in the wall originally designed for cross-ventilation, and now enlarged into small windows to provide surprise peeks at the landscape. There's also a smooth steel-faced cylinder evoking a silo (opposite page); there is a real silo on the opposite side, but it's empty and may see use at a future date to store wine. The cylinder houses a mudroom at ground level and a bathroom above.

The tricky challenge of connecting the new structure with the picturesque original is shown at its most imaginative in the great central atrium (following pages). Leading off the living level are small reading and study spaces, with sliding doors left mostly in the open position but available for privacy. The most dramatic gesture is a bold steel and glass bridge (you can see the underside, top right, following pages). The bridge connects the generous master bedroom, with its southern exposure, to the bath and dressing spaces. The intent was to preserve the lightness of the open space by moving bedroom and bathroom to opposite ends of the house and not obstructing the central atrium.

The owners enjoyed every moment of the experience. Says Kathleen Martin: "The process was as exciting as the building. There were no fights with the architect. We imposed no ideas on him." The architects had designed an earlier house for them back in San Francisco—a converted warehouse that gave their high-tech leanings full sway. This time, the challenge was different. Yet the result manages to distill the best out of two contrasting styles. Oddly enough, it's the Modern, with its lucid, crisp, cool use of industrial materials and sharp forms, that has the upper hand. *Stephen A. Kliment*

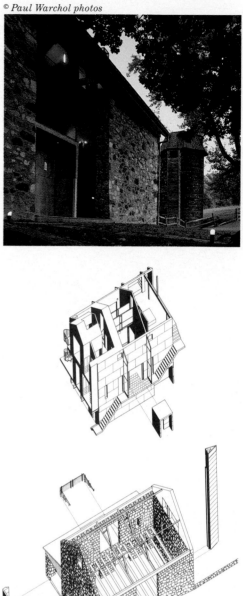

Main entry to the 3,500-square-feet barn-turned-residence is through a metal box that penetrates the 20-inch rough stone walls (top). The architects inserted a cherrywood-finished, self-supporting box inside the old stone barn (drawings, above), with the space between the two for circulation. Ancient wind-eyes were enlarged to become windows (opposite). The steel-coated silo-like cylinder contains a mudroom, with a bathroom above.

A central atrium connects the three levels (far left and opposite page). Boxy chairs and a coffee table are by the architects, and are supplemented by early American heirlooms such as a bench, a hinged table, and bookstands. Frequent entertaining occurs on the lower level (left and lower left). The kitchen is separated from dining by a custom-made metal-framed glass partition, with a cantilevered granite serving surface. Access to a large barbecuing terrace is through the stone wall to the left in lower photo. The house is heated by radiant hot water—partly by vertical panels, partly by pipes embedded in the lower level floor. Water is piped from a natural spring shared with two neighbors.

Credits
Martin Residence
Kennett Square, Pennsylvania
Owners: *David and Kathleen Martin*
Architect: *Tenner Leddy Maytum Stacy Architects—William Leddy, partner-in-charge; Craig Edwards, job captain; Joanne Kennedy, Douglas Gauthier, Kim Kwan, project team*
Engineers: *Robert Chagnon (structural); Gary Debes (mechanical)*
General Contractor: *Mobac, Inc.*

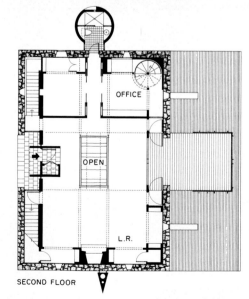

FIRST FLOOR

MUD RM.

D.R.

L.R.

SECOND FLOOR

OFFICE

OPEN

L.R.

THIRD FLOOR

M. BATH

OPEN   OPEN

M. BR

N

6 FT
2 M.

The program was deceptively simple: a modest-sized structure with enough space for guests, a painting studio, and holiday gatherings that would complement a 19th-century farmhouse on a 100-acre property in upstate New York. Architects Deborah Berke and Carey McWhorter's response blends with farmyard vernacular without aping it, thanks to the rigorous purity of its forms. Clients Peter Halley and Caroline Stewart's requirements initially seemed at odds with each other. He, a painter and leading proponent of the "Neo Geo" movement, grew up in a cramped Manhattan apartment craving wide-open loft space. She, raised on a Louisiana plantation, wanted a traditional farm compound and a porch. The architects accommodated them both within 1,500 square feet and a tight budget.

The hillside site facing the Berkshires is in the path of run-off streamlets, which created water-drainage complications. The architects constructed an arching curtain drain; filled with rocks and gravel, it draws water around the house before it resumes its course to a pond downhill. To anchor the structure, Berke and McWhorter set the north end into the gradually rising slope, merging building and land much the same way as the main house burrows into the hill. Only the lawn in front of the porch was leveled to create added usable outdoor living space.

The house is a three-part volume comprising porch, studio, and bedrooms. Materials are limited to shingles, sheetrock, plywood, and tongue-and-groove joined pine, but are used differently to express each of the parts. The studio is clad in shingles with four 8-foot 6-inch windows set flush into the eastern facade; by contrast, the guest house has vertical siding with 16-inch-deep window sills. The porch facade, topped by a cathedral-ceilinged bedroom, is the most complex composition. Here, the window sill of the gable intersects the wood framing of the porch, which rises above the base of the upper floor to dramatize its nonstructural role.

While the exterior clearly suggests a condensed farm compound, the interior has the spaciousness of a loft combined with the simplicity of a Shaker meeting house. Given the straightforward plan, there is a richness in the careful detailing and spatial contrasts. For example, the porch does not enter directly into the large studio; instead, passage is interrupted by a hall that turns into a staircase, its slow rise paralleling the nearby hill. The staircase to the bedroom over the porch appears to be cut out of the wall (opposite bottom); its steep grade is reminiscent of kitchen stairs in New England farmhouses. A sequence of two guest bedrooms and a bath off a long hall at the top of the graduated stair completes the plan. In these rooms, the windows, though smaller than those in the studio, admit generous east and west light.

Berke and McWhorter relied on such old-fashioned ventilation methods as high ceilings and small windows, and sited the house to take advantage of two shade trees. It is with such seemingly conventional gestures that the architects reveal the power of simplicity.
Julie Iovine

Julie Iovine is a New York City-based freelance writer.

Credits
Studio/Guest House
Hillsdale, New York
Owners: *Peter Halley and Caroline Stewart*
Architect: *Deborah Berke and Carey McWhorter, Architects*
General Contractor: *Shadic Builders, Inc.*

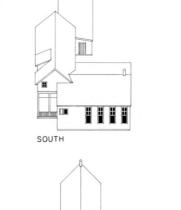

SOUTH

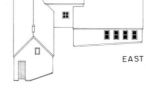

EAST

WEST

NORTH

PORCH

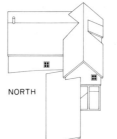

HALL   STUDY

STUDIO

→N

6 FT.
2 M.

Berke and McWhorter achieved the effect of a compound by interlocking three volumes with distinct functions. The porch elevation (opposite, top and center) has a single gable, while a shed-roofed portion (opposite, bottom) of the building contains two guest bedrooms and a bath. The architects originally envisioned a single large window for the studio/gathering room, but their client artist Peter Halley said that he preferred windows like those in New England Congregational churches (top). Two stairs meet on a landing between studio and the guest-bedroom wing (bottom).

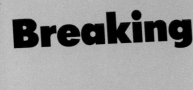

Breaking

Though the house shown in these pages hardly looks experimental, it is the culmination of a 10-year exploratory process by Bentley LaRosa Salasky. The partners departed early from their minimalist roots, and the work is now neither archeological traditionalism nor tied to the trend of the moment—a quality that intrigued the clients. "What always comes up when Postmodernism is debated is that people are comfortable with tradition," says Ron Bentley. "But people also want what Modernism offers—large expanses of glass, interlocking space, outdoor orientation." The architects haven't chosen one approach over the other, Bentley explains. "We try to make people comfortable, yet work with [Modern] aspirations."

Having long and often walked the four-acre site together, the clients asked the architects to tuck the house into the highest corner to command a sweep of greenery studded with mature specimen trees and shrubs planted by a previous owner. (Landscape architect Billie Cohen collaborated in the substantial editing effort.) To take advantage of this "garden gone wild," the architects found inspiration in the "butterfly" plans drawn by turn-of-the-century English architects to unify house and landscape for a then-new suburban clientele. Bentley LaRosa Salasky's version anchors the house to its site with a central block containing the main living areas; the wings are hinged to form a graveled auto court to the west and reach into the expansive garden to the east. The visitor sees the house obliquely both entering and leaving (opposite top). This "picturesque" experience emphasizes the design's abstract, geometric qualities—a distinctly "Modern" experience.

The punched, symmetrical windows and massive, attenuated chimneys of the central block (suggestive of country-house antecedents) counter the horizontal proportions, low-sloped hip roofs with deep eaves, and glazed and carved-away corners, all of which bring to mind Prairie-School Frank Lloyd Wright (preceding pages). As with Wright, there is a constant interplay between exterior and interior. The living room, exaggerated in the house's massing, commands the most sweeping view. In plan, the room is a simple rectangle, but the architects have left the corners open, leading the eye to the complex interlocking spaces beyond, and permitting fingers of sunlight to penetrate indirectly virtually any time of the day.

In details, there is also a tension between Modern and traditional. The symmetry of the main volume is emphasized through its hipped roof and vertical board-on-board siding. Yet this same volume is visually pulled apart by the overscaled window wall at the entry (top photo) and eroded by the curve in the bow-windowed den (opposite top). The house evokes but never quotes. At every turn, says Sal LaRosa, "We asked, can we transform this element, imbue it with another life?"

Equally at home with decoration and architecture, the designers developed and restated themes at an extraordinary variety of scales. A custom chandelier, reworked, is a sconce. Japanese proportioned "French" curves defined a family of profiles used for crown moldings, a fireplace mantel, column capitals, and cabinet tops; it's turned vertically for wood "linenfold" paneling. Likewise, painted exterior wood columns reappear on the interior, slightly altered in proportion and lovingly detailed in oak and mahogany with a "capital" of wrapped copper wire. The near-obsessive scope of the design seems at odds with the words the architects use to describe what they hoped to achieve: "simplicity," "composed," "unself-conscious." That this house looks like it has always been there—while looking like no other—testifies to their success. *James S. Russell*

The Westchester house is intended to be seen from an angle (opposite top), though the frontal view best explains its relation of parts to whole (preceding pages). Viewed from a separate painting studio, an overscaled window wall signals the entrance (top). Deep overhangs emphasize the horizontal in the master-bedroom wing (opposite bottom). By carefully arranging stepped terraces and stone-faced walls, the architects protected the garden-side pool (above) without fencing it in.

STUDIO

SECOND FLOOR

BR.

BR

BR.

The open, flowing plan is overlaid with subtly developed axes: from entry to master bedroom, from dining to den. Paired columns supporting a roof over a terrace draw the eye through a dining nook to the landscape (opposite top left). A copper fascia and Arts and Crafts tiles transform a Wrightian device, the double-facing fireplace (opposite bottom). Details such as columns, molding profiles, and light fixtures recur, subtly rescaled in the den (opposite top right), the entry (top left), and the upstairs corridor (left). Compare, for example, the oak column and a leg of the custom Windsor chair.

Credits

Westchester Residence
Westchester County, New York
Architect: *Bentley LaRosa Salasky, Architects and Decorators—Ronald Bentley, Salvatore LaRosa, Franklin Salasky, partners-in-charge; Peter Dick, Denise De Coster, Benjamin Benson, Adam Rolston, Jylle Menoff, J. Robert Yogel, Lana Hum, Joseph Morrison, Jean Krueger, project team*
Engineers: *Robert Silman Associates (structural); Regis Engineering (mechanical)*
Landscape Architect: *A. Billie Cohen*
Contractors: *Franco Brothers (general); John Skovron (landscape)*

KIT.

D.R.

L. R.

DEN

M. BR.

GAR.

FIRST FLOOR

10 FT.

3 M.

The house that Frank Israel renovated for Howard Goldberg and Jim Bean in the Hollywood hills is an attention-getter, even by Los Angeles standards. This will please those familiar with the original—a 2,400-square-foot 1950s bungalow on a 1/2-acre lot in the Outpost section of the "hills"—which lacked the sort of distinction suggested by the site. But like his clients, Goldberg, a talent agent, and Bean, a real-estate investor, Israel recognized potential. By adding a foyer/gallery and a master bedroom tower, totaling 1,550 square feet, and recladding the existing structure, the architect made the undistinguished ranch into a star.

Development of Outpost, a planned community, began in the 1920s and design regulations governing use of building materials virtually mandated a neighborhood style of Spanish revival. In recent years, the regulations, which architects considered stifling, have been mostly repealed, yielding a new but uneven crop of houses. In remaking the Goldberg-Bean house, Israel chose not to erase local history but rather to embellish it. An assiduous analyst of architecture with a special interest in the California building tradition, Israel is quick to point out various references in his work. Shiplap cedar siding on the new front gate, for example, is meant to recall the house's previous lapped siding. The new mustard-colored stucco finish and reddish cedar cladding was inspired by the bright hues of original Outpost buildings. "Looking around the neighborhood you realize that in terms of color, this house is contextual," says Israel.

Israel purposely casts a wide referential net. Discussing the layout of the rooms, he cites the Case Study Houses, the subject of "Blueprints for Modern Living," a major exhibition at the Los Angeles Museum of Contemporary Art held prior to the Goldberg-Bean commission, as a bench mark of the city's cultural identity and his own professional development. The Case Study prototype, where interior and exterior spaces seem to merge into one barrier-free living area, is evident in the new floor plan, which Israel conceived with project architect Steven Shortridge. By opening up the old living room with new sliding glass doors that lead to the backyard and then on to paved terraces that step down to the swimming pool (opposite top), inside and outside merge into one. The architects removed a row of mature shrubs along the narrow site's western edge, where it dramatically drops 50 feet to reveal views of the city below. They also sharpened the contours close to the edge to further intensify the feeling of boundless space.

Whereas the west elevation opens to the garden and the city beyond, the east elevation presents a protected public face to the street (previous pages). Here, openings are few and serve more to admit eastern light than to provide views; even the recessed entrance is screened by a glass and steel canopy. The tower is aligned on axis with a perpendicular street, creating a visual hinge in the 150-foot-long street facade. The great length's effect is lessened by the use of contrasting materials, a solution seemingly influenced by Frank Gehry. Israel agrees that he, too, wants "to emphasize the various pieces," but unlike Gehry he eschews material "collisions" in favor of crafted joints, similar, in his mind, to the work of Italian master Carlo Scarpa. Joints are indeed meticulous: redwood battens accent the tower's cedar panel modules, Douglas fir delineates window frames, and terra cotta tile on the roof distinguishes "old" house from "new," echoing the tile once mandated by Outpost rules. Tying the pavilions together is a 90-foot-long blue stucco wall that begins inside as a fireplace surround (following pages), and then curves through the foyer to emerge boldly at the house's north corner—a sweeping gesture worthy of Hollywood. *Karen D. Stein*

Since local zoning regulations did not require a setback from the street, Israel's 1,550-square-foot addition to an existing 2,400-square-foot 1950s ranch closely follows the curving frontage (site plan above). The entrance is, however, recessed in a forecourt and screened from public view and the sun by a steel and sandblasted-glass canopy (previous pages). A glass gallery, the link between the existing bungalow and the new tower master-bedroom suite (opposite), separates the foyer from the backyard. The architect used different materials to express the various forms: cedar plywood with redwood battens on the tower, bonderized sheet metal on the curved master bedroom wall and chimney, and a light-sand-finished mustard-colored stucco on the forms between.

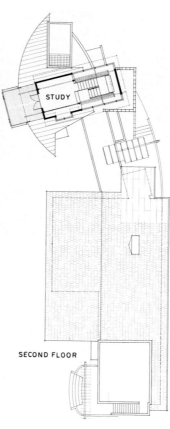

STUDY

SECOND FLOOR

M. BR.

N

LIVING-DINING

K.

BR.

FIRST FLOOR

10 FT.

3 M.

BR.

A 90-foot-long curved blue-pigmented stucco wall with a smooth, steel-troweled finish ties the existing house to Israel's addition, emerging at the north corner. The blue wall separates the living room from an expanded kitchen (opposite top) and creates a light-filled gallery that links public rooms with the more private master bedroom suite (opposite bottom and following pages). The master bedroom is dominated by a built-in "two-poster" bed with two steel columns supporting Douglas fir gluelam beams (bottom left). Exposed floor joists of the study above (top left) form the "canopy." The study's balcony shades the master bedroom, while deep eaves shade the living room and adjacent porch.

Credits

Goldberg-Bean House
Los Angeles, California
Owners: Howard Goldberg and Jim Bean
Architect: Franklin D. Israel Design Associates—Franklin D. Israel, principal-in-charge; Steven S. Shortridge, project architect; James Simeo, Danny Kaplan, Jeffrey Chusid, Leslie Shapiro, and Michael Poris, project team
Engineers: M. B. & A. (mechanical); Davis Design Group (structural)
Consultants: Jay Griffith (landscape); F. I. R. E. Ltd. (lighting); Future Home (audio/visual)
General Contractor: A. R. T.—Lawrence Garcia

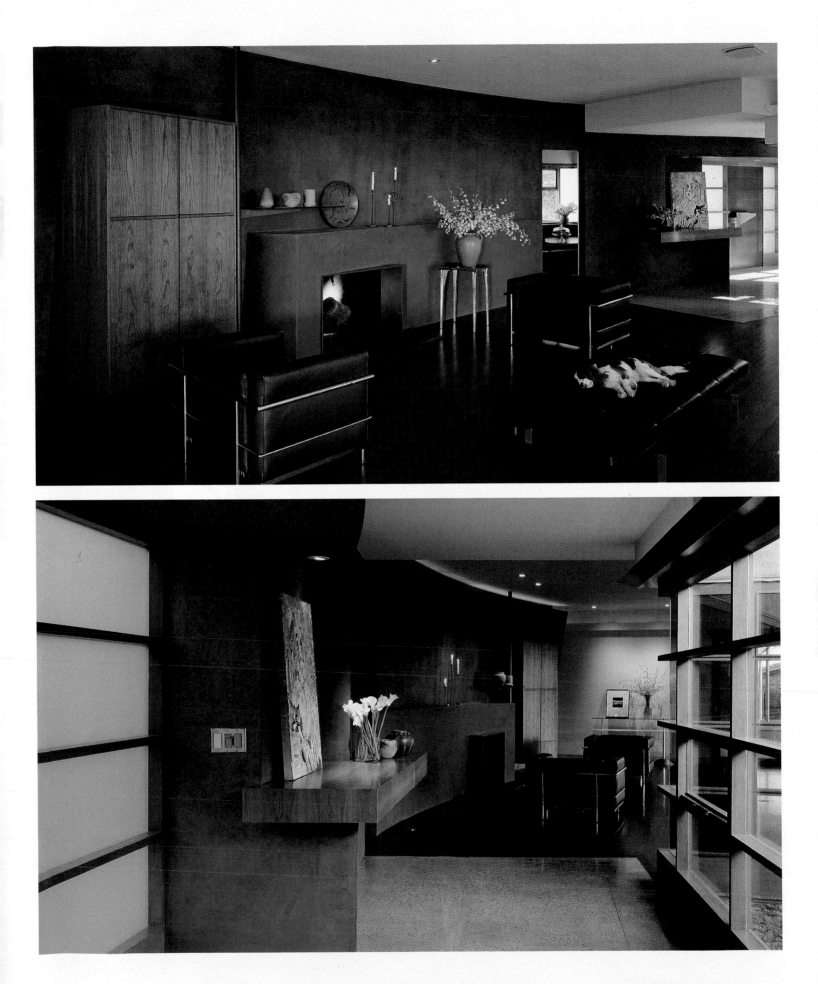

TECHNOLOGY FOCUS:
Stairway Details

As editors, we spend a considerable time getting to know each project we write about. We become privy to the intense effort that goes into making what may appear on our pages as simple and obvious. A window surround, a roof edge, a cabinetry profile may not assert itself in the design, yet can often be, as a friend says, a poem. Thus, we inaugurate this occasional series in which we show only details. Stairs make a worthy subject, especially within RECORD HOUSES, since they lend themselves to endless interpretation. This group has been chosen to represent a range

Westchester House

*Westchester County, New York
Bentley LaRosa Salasky,
Architects and Decorators*

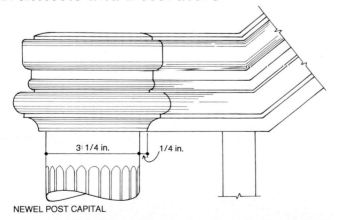

5 1/8 in.
1 in.
2 1/2 in.
1 1/4 in.

BALUSTER BOARD

© Michael Mundy photos

Addition to a House

*Westchester County, New York
Bentley LaRosa Salasky,
Architects and Decorators*

3 1/4 in.
1/4 in.

NEWEL POST CAPITAL

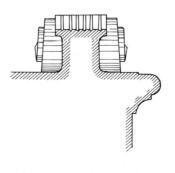

SECTION THROUGH HANDRAIL

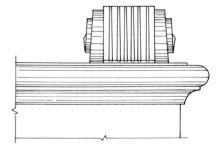

END OF HANDRAIL

of budgets as well as styles. Note that assembling details in one story by type is an old idea we're bringing back. In March 1938, when RECORD incorporated AMERICAN ARCHITECT AND ARCHITECTURE, it began running that publication's portfolios of details (the first was rain leaders). It's still a fresh idea 55 years later. J. S. R.

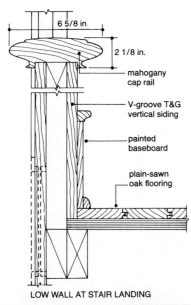

6 5/8 in.

2 1/8 in.

mahogany cap rail

V-groove T&G vertical siding

painted baseboard

plain-sawn oak flooring

LOW WALL AT STAIR LANDING

Tight corner

Stair details for this house (shown on pages 94-99) restate themes developed throughout the design. The round newel posts are members of a "family" of columns, which occur at various locations. The architects adjusted the thickness and degree of entasis to suit each column's height. Likewise, the baluster of the open rail (plan detail opposite left) is a variation on profiles devised for moldings and trim. Unusually high, the stair stringer's dimension was designed to achieve a pleasing balustrade proportion. Prior to fabrication, woodworkers laid out the stair in their shop to verify that the curved shapes would fit together. A solid balustrade (attached to the lower newel post in far left photo but not visible) is clad in painted vertical beaded-board (detail, near left) as an extension of an adjacent wainscoted surface. ■

© Andrew Garn photos

Classical return

An existing stair had to be redesigned for an addition and remodeling that included creating a double-height entry hall within an existing envelope. The architects stayed with the classical French style of the house in designing the addition. Though treads and risers were retained, an open balustrade was designed incorporating three different thinly proportioned one-and-one-half-inch diameter balusters. Two are weighted more heavily to the bottom; one to the middle. The architects had seen such baluster combinations elsewhere. "We liked the interplay," comments partner Ron Bentley. From the newel post (detail opposite far left), a double-molding rail follows the balustrade up the stair, along the length of a balcony (near right photo) to a solid balustrade-cum-bookcase. The upper half of the rail profile ends in a scroll molding (opposite middle and right detail), while the lower half matches the profile of the bookcase's top. Another solid balustrade curves out of the wall; by carrying the paneling from the adjacent surface, it was treated as an extension of the wall into the space (left photo). ■

Alldredge House

Glen Arbor, Michigan; Charles Warren, Architect

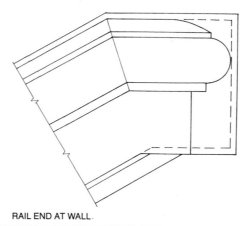

RAIL END AT WALL.

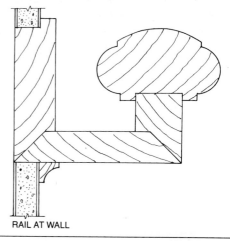

RAIL AT WALL

Cooper Bauer Apartment

Boston, Massachusetts
Denison Luchini, Architect

Photo courtesy *Metropolitan Home*

Davis Rosenthal House

Lyme, Connecticut
Scot P. Samuelson, Architect

George Ross photos

Prairie Piranesi

With its intricate route, this stair evokes the picturesque vistas and intimate inglenooks of late-19th-century houses. Indirect sun from small dormer windows lights the lowest level. Light spilling down from a viewing tower leads the visitor up. The house's split-level scheme places the main floor a half level above grade for views over dunes to Lake Michigan. The stair is "sort of Piranesian," says architect Charles Warren. "From any one of the house's levels you can see the other ones." The level changes also separate the master bedroom suite from rooms for guests (near left). The bolted connections and simple joinery were inspired by forms found in rural Michigan. Warren has detailed the stair rail so that dropped posts divide panels of round and square balusters (left). The handrail profile (opposite left) is carried on wood brackets where the stair passes between walls (opposite right). ■

HANDRAIL ELEVATION

1 ft

7 ft 6 1/2 in.

3 ft 9 in.

R = 3 ft 7 in.

3 ft

3 ft

Compound curves

Stairs connecting three levels are the star of an apartment renovation within a loftlike old mill building. "Our attitude," said partner Dirk Denison, "was to get back to the wonderful texture and surfaces of the original buildng." The lowest stair is even penetrated by an existing building column. A mix of wood, sealed weathering steel, and brass, the stair rails have multiple trajectories. "We wanted the things we added to read as interventions," explains Denison. Adjacent (but separated from) the wall, a partly wood-capped curved metal rail springs from the base of the lower stair. After a gap, it's completed by another rail using a different radius (drawing left and photo opposite). On the open side of the stair, a steel balustrade, capped by a brass rail and infilled with metal mesh, flows parallel to stair treads. The architects added curved ramps at the top of the bottom flight and the bottom of the top flight. Metal rails are welded, and tongue-and-groove wood treads are bolted to steel stringers. The "self-consciousness" of the details is intended, says Denison, "to make people acutely sensitized to the environment and the way that they interact with it." ■

Shakeresque stair tower

Site restrictions mandated a narrow footprint for this small house (less than 1,300 square feet) for a couple with children. Architect Scot Samuelson pulled stairs out of the structure's main body and placed them in a tower. "With a house this small, the staircase becomes big in proportion to the rest of the house," he explains. "By getting the stair out of the center of activity, I felt I could get a better use of space." Responding to both a modest budget and a minimal fee, Samuelson produced an intriguing result with minimum means: carefully placed windows (taking advantage of water views), natural-finished yellow pine stair treads, and beaded-board tongue-and-groove cedar cladding. Cedar cap rails and newel posts have a Shaker-style simplicity. ■

PRESERVATION
PLAN ON IT

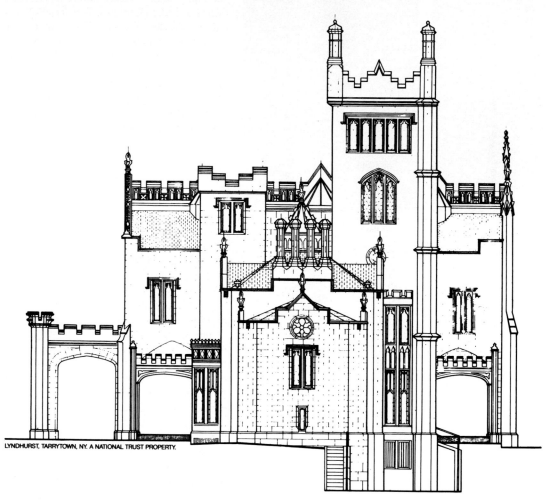

LYNDHURST, TARRYTOWN, NY. A NATIONAL TRUST PROPERTY.

Planning on restoring a house, saving a landmark, reviving your neighborhood?

No matter what your plans, gain a wealth of experience and help preserve our historic and architectural heritage. Join the National Trust for Historic Preservation and support preservation efforts in your community.

Make preservation a blueprint for the future.

Write:

**National Trust for Historic Preservation
Department PA
1785 Massachusetts Ave., N.W.
Washington, D.C. 20036**

Manufacturer Sources

For your convenience in locating building materials and other products shown in this month's feature articles, RECORD has asked the architects to identify the products specified.

Pages 64-71
Theuer Residence
William P. Bruder, Architect
Metal panels, gate, stainless-steel fireplace, and perforated-metal sunshade: Lewis Machine and Welding. Glass (windows and entrance): PPG Industries, Glass Group (Solex). Hardware and push bars: The Ironmonger, Inc. Aluminum patio chairs: Knoll International (Pesci). Bath lighting and low-voltage recessed lights: Halo. Sink: American Standard. Tile: Endicott. Switches: Leviton. Chrome chairs: Knoll International. Custom maple-veneer plywood doors, windows, and maple-batten ceiling: Laurent Construction. Refrigerator: Amana Refrigeration.

Pages 72-75
Artist's Studio and Residence
Tigerman McCurry, Architect
Stucco: La Habra Stucco. Aluminum-clad wood windows and French doors: Peachtree. Lever-handle locksets: Schlage. Glass: Twinsul. Corrugated-aluminum roofing: Industrial Building Panels. Ceiling fan: McMaster Carr. Track lighting fixtures: Halo. Paints: Dunn Edwards. Integral-color concrete: Ready-Mix, Inc.

Pages 76-83
Gorman Residence
Hariri & Hariri Design, Architects
Steel windows and doors: A&S Window Associates. Stucco: Thoro System Products. Standing-seam roof: Berridge Mfg. (Galvalume). Modified-bitumen roofing: U.S. Intec. Paints: Benjamin Moore & Co. Garage doors: Finishline Ind., Inc. Exterior sconces: Poulsen Lighting, Inc. (Skot Wall). Entrance metalwork: Scott Madison. Locksets: OMNIA Industries, Inc. Fenestra Limestone flooring: Innovative Marble. Ceiling fixtures: CSL Lighting. Pivot hinges, cabinet pulls: Stanley. Self-closing hinges: Grass. Stainless-steel countertop: Lab Fabricators Co. Faucets: Speakman. Stove: Viking. Refrigerator: Traulsen.

Pages 84-89
Martin Residence
Tanner Leddy Maytum Stacy Architects
Metal cladding: Lead-coated copper. Spotlighting and recessed fixtures: Lightolier and Halo. Living-room club chairs and tables: designed by William Leddy, TLMS. MR16 spots: Arteluce. Radiator: Runtal North America, Inc. Obscure glass at interior: Page Glass, Inc. Lever-handle locksets: The Ironmonger (D Line). Exterior lighting: BEGA/FS, Lumiere. Pulls on kitchen cabinets: Forms+Surfaces. Ceiling lights: Poulsen Lighting, Inc. Skylights: O'Keeffes, Inc. Wood sculptures: Kathleen Edwards.

Pages 90-93
Studio/Guest House
Deborah Berke and Carey McWhorter, Architects
Shingle roofing: Bird, Inc. Exterior opaque stain: Samuel Cabot, Inc. (Red Barn). Awning and double-hung windows, patio door: Marvin Windows. Paints: Dutch Boy. Entrance, interior and sliding doors, cabinetwork: custom by architects, fabricated by Shadic Builders, Inc. Hardware: Schlage Lock Co.

Pages 94-99
Westchester Residence
Bentley LaRosa Salasky, Architects and Decorators
Shingles: GAF (Timberline). Exterior stucco: Bonsal (Marblesil). Windows: Marvin Windows. Exterior sconces: Poulsen Lighting, Inc. (Orbiter). Switchplates: Lutron. Doors and cabinet hardware: Baldwin Brass. Countertops: Formica Corp. Carpeting: Stark. Paint: Benjamin Moore & Co. White-oak paneling: Breakfast Woodworks. Pendant light in breakfast nook: Scandinavian Design. Other fixtures: custom by architects, fabricated by Wainlands. Wood blinds: Levelor, Inc. Stone-flag flooring: Pennsylvania Bluestone. Fireplace tile: EPRO.

Pages 100-107
Goldberg-Bean Residence
Franklin D. Israel Design Associates, Architect
Mosaic and pool tile: American-Olean Tile. Windows: custom by architect. Roofing: U.S. Intec. Locksets: Baldwin. Master-bedroom fireplace: custom plaster and steel-plate hearth and mantel by architect; prefabricated firebox. Integral-color concrete: Suncrete.

1994

Building Types Study 715/Record Houses 1994

Record Houses should be subtitled "The houses we love (including some our readers love to hate.)" Each year the editors solicit and review several hundred submissions before selecting winners. Invariably, there's dissent in the ranks as the process begins. But once we narrow the field to a group of some 20 finalists, a consensus begins to emerge. Although the eight projects shown here represent a wide range of clients, sites, programs, and budgets, all possess a unique quality of imagination that makes them stand out, along with the highest level of execution. Each of us has a favorite—the house we want (this year) as our own—and we defend our choices as if they expressed a profound personal vision. A previous editor of Record Houses once compared eccentric houses to eccentric people, commenting that they "can be uncommonly engaging or insufferable beyond measure. One's response often depends on whether the singular phenomenon, human or architectural, seems spontaneously original or self-consciously bizarre." Looking back, we've certainly published both, and our readers are among the first to point out which they think is which. We've come to savor the fact that over time some of the most hated houses have become the best loved; that intense reaction contains the power to provoke and teach.
Karen D. Stein

Manufacturers' Sources listed on page 129

The beach front "casita," a two-story, two-room structure, functions as an interior design studio for the client and as a guest and beach house. Almost a cube (it is 15 feet long by 15 feet wide and 18 feet tall), it has a roof that slants up towards the sea. It is a concrete, steel, and glass structure with panoramic views looking northeast onto the Atlantic Ocean. The casita is protected from the full force of the sun by an innovative copper shield that can be raised and lowered with a key switch, similar to a light switch, tied into a hydraulic system. The side and back walls are unfenestrated stucco on concrete block to focus views toward the sea.

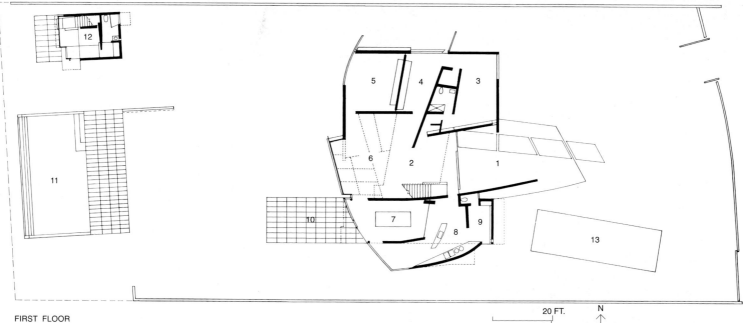

FIRST FLOOR

20 FT.

6 M.

N

Zapata and West used stainless steel in three forms (wire, beaded and polished) throughout the house. Concrete stair treads were covered with beaded stainless; the railing is polished steel strung with wire cable. The door to the kitchen is also beaded stainless steel. In many cases, poured-in-place concrete walls were left untouched. In the foyer, the floor is the same blue-green serpentine used on the terrace and pool coping. Other floors are covered in mahogany , maple, and sisal.

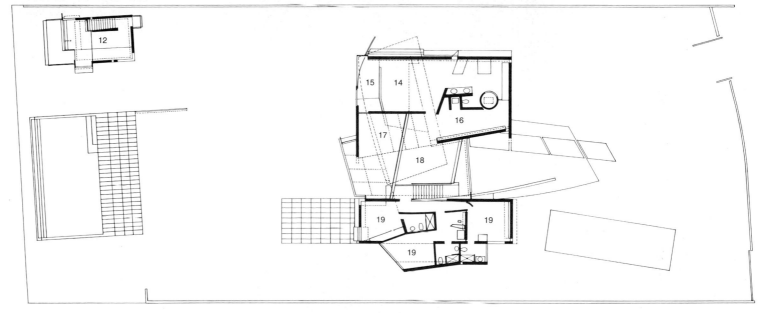

SECOND FLOOR

1. Lily pond
2. Foyer
3. Den/guest room
4. Garden room
5. Study
6. Living room
7. Dining room
8. Kitchen
9. Laundry
10. Outdoor dining

11. Pool
12. Guest house
13. Proposed garage
14. Master bedroom
15. Terrace
16. Gym
17. Open
18. Family room
19. Bedroom

Ga

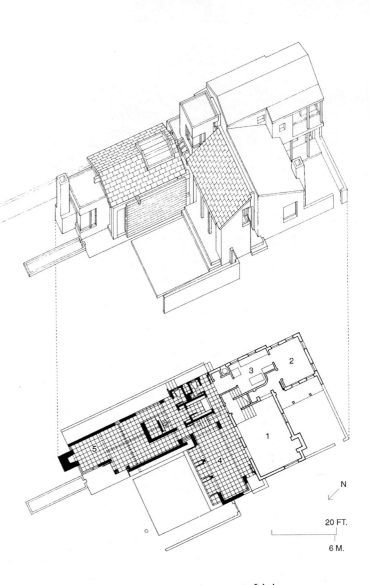

"They are like relatives," says Susan Lanier of the 1920s Spanish Colonial style house and its recent addition in west Los Angeles. "But of different generations," adds partner Paul Lubowicki. While old and new have a family likeness—thick white-painted plaster walls and a clear distinction between materials—each has its own identity. "I didn't want any period associations," explains owner Susan Stringfellow of the careful blending of parts into an eclectic yet seamless whole. In fact, the mix of existing structure and new construction emphasizes not any historical era, but the dual nature of the house: public rooms facing the street and private areas oriented toward a lush garden and reflecting pond in the back. In a twist on convention, the architects have made the most "private" room, the master-bedroom-suite, the largest and most open room in the house.

Lubowicki and Lanier's 1,100-square-foot L-shaped addition nearly doubles the size of the house, pushing the structure 55 feet into the backyard. The architects reduced the effect of the new volume by lowering it one foot into the ground. Working with landscape architect Nancy Powers, they surrounded the bedroom with large gravel, creating a rock garden. The new gallery/dining room is separated from the patio by two steps—a deliberately prolonged transition between inside and outside that Lubowicki calls "the period of doubt." Its lead-coated copper roof makes the old shed roof into a gable (drawing right).

The master bedroom is itself an amalgam of parts carefully arranged to control views in and out. In the center of the composition is the shower, left open on the south to the side yard and topped by a skylight. A gently-sloped gable floats overhead, projecting beyond exterior walls. Sleeping and sitting areas are punctured by a massive 5-foot 3-inch cube fireplace of sandblasted concrete, which terminates the loft-like space like a giant exclamation point (previous pages). "It amplifies your experience of outdoors," explains Lubowicki of this exhibitionistic use of glass. Stringfellow sleeps at times in the renovated "old" bedroom, calling the cramped quarters "cozy," but considers herself "transformed" by her spacious garden wing that occupies the "magical land" carefully landscaped into overgrown flower beds and meandering pathways by Powers.

This house is Lubowicki and Lanier's first finished project since forming their own practice in 1988. While five years between design and completion seems long, it allowed the architects to continuously refine their scheme. "It's as bottom-line as you can get," says Lubowicki of the material connections. "There's nothing extraneous; each part is clear." "The barrier is reduced," explains Lanier of the previous separation between house and garden, and she says of the addition, "it doesn't impose itself on you." *Karen D. Stein*

N

20 FT.

6 M.

1. *Living room*
2. *Study*
3. *Kitchen*
4. *Dining room*
5. *Bedroom*

© *Tom Bonner photos*

Two sets of French doors mark the transition from old house to new (top left and bottom left). During a delay between design and construction, Susan Lanier and Paul Lubowicki refined the parts and material connections of their structure. The steel frame of the bedroom is clearly delineated from a poured-in-place concrete wall that has the grain-like pattern and striations from the 2-inch by 8-inch planks of its wood formwork. Laminated wood beams are separated from steel beams by custom-made brackets and burst through glass to the outside (top right and bottom right). Floors are French limestone.

Credits
Stringfellow Residence
Los Angeles, California
Owner: *Susan Stringfellow*
Architect: *Lubowicki/Lanier Architects—Susan Lanier, partner-in-charge; Feliciano Reyes, Jr., project architect; David Spinelli, Ben Ball, project team*

Engineers: *Gordon Polon (structural); Bill Comeau (mechanical)*
Consultant: *Nancy Powers & Associates (landscape)*
General Contractor: *Alexander Construction*

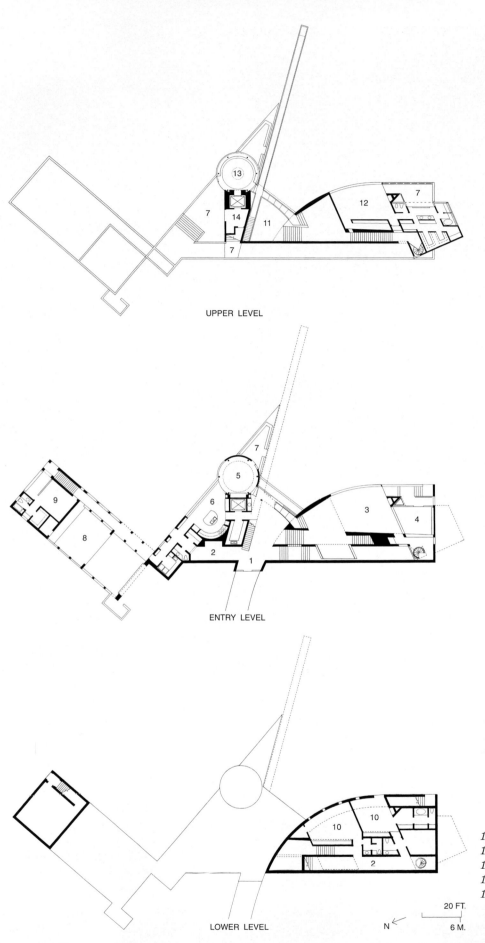

UPPER LEVEL

ENTRY LEVEL

LOWER LEVEL

To take full advantage of the site overlooking a picturesque ravine, Predock designed the house to enhance casual encounters with the outdoors. To this end he provided access to outdoor spaces from almost every room in the house and turned the roof into an adult playground for dining, entertaining, and birdwatching. On the third level, the circular dining room leads directly out to a dining terrace with a built-in catering station (opposite top left). Wrap-around windows and a circular skylight give occupants of the dining room a sense of floating in the trees (opposite middle right). Directly above the dining room, visitors can lounge outside or even walk across the skylight (opposite top right).

An indoor bridge stretches along the house's glazed east wall and links the living room to the dining room (opposite middle left). A terrace lets residents circulate around the outside of the house (opposite bottom left). One of the most dramatic features of the house is its metal-framed, cable-stabilized skyramp that juts over the sloped ravine to offer spectacular views (opposite bottom right).

Floor plans show the three major levels (left). However, a number of spaces in the house—both indoors and out—fall on intermediate levels, adding an organizational complexity found in many Predock buildings.

1. Entry
2. Art hall
3. Living
4. Library
5. Den
6. Kitchen
7. Deck/terrace
8. Garage
9. Grandmother's suite
10. Bedroom
11. Open
12. Master bedroom
13. Dining
14. Catering station

20 FT.

N

6 M.

Although just 2,400 square feet, the von Stein House works as an entire village—with a series of structures climbing a hillside site and a rich variety of indoor and outdoor spaces. As in some European villages, movement through the house is often circuitous but never confusing. Winding your way around, under, and through the small buildings, you discover the architecture in pieces and realize that the spaces between are as important as the buildings themselves.

Designed for a married couple who split their time between Germany and California, the house combines the clients' love of Modernism with their desire to build in keeping with the architectural traditions of northern California. "This house is more abstract than some of our earlier work," explains architect Laura Hartman. "Instead of using vernacular forms, we followed vernacular strategies." In plan the house appears to be essentially Modern, with a trio of rectangular courtyards emanating from a linear spine. But in elevation the picturesque forms of vernacular architecture are more apparent: towers of different heights, trellises, and pitched roofs. In selecting materials, the architects also blended Modern with traditional— combining concrete block and metal sun shades with clapboard and wooden battens.

From the driveway and carport located at the bottom of the site, one walks under redwood trellises and up a series of steps that leads around the front court, under the main tower, and into the central courtyard. Although this tiled inner court doesn't have the outdoor fireplace originally envisioned for it (see axonometric below), it does offer dramatic views of the Valley of the Moon to the southeast, and serves as an important "room" at the heart of the house. At the rear of the site is what Richard Fernau calls "the philosopher's garden," a gravel court that provides pacing room or sunning space for those staying in the adjacent guest tower.

Underscoring the idea of the house as a set of buildings pieced together to form a community, fragments of some buildings emerge on the inside of others. For example, the corner of the main tower— complete with exterior wood siding—pushes its way inside the kitchen, and the master bedroom suite sits above the living room as if it were a freestanding structure built inside the house.

A wood-frame structure built on a poured-concrete foundation and within concrete retaining walls, the von Stein House grows out of its hillside site. And with its courtyards and gardens and towertops offering sun and views to the valley below, the house is fully engaged with its surroundings. *Clifford A. Pearson*

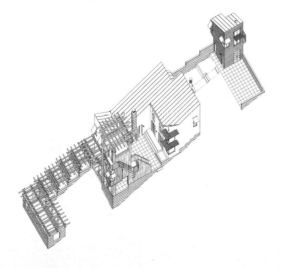

© *Richard Barnes photos*

At the bottom of the hill, concrete stairs and a redwood trellis define the spine of the house and also establish the pattern of outdoor rooms alternating with indoor ones (top). At the top of the site, gravel and a low wall give the "philosopher's garden" a different char- acter from other outdoor spaces (middle). Sun shades on the southeast side of the house are made from standard metal grating (above). The inner court is the heart of the house (opposite).

Suit to a T

T-House
Wilton, New York
Simon Ungers and Tom Kinslow,
Architects

A house says a lot about who you are," claims Lawrence Marcelle. Although the T-House, named for the way it configures living space and library into two rectangular blocks stacked perpendicularly atop one another, might not fully represent its owner, an aspiring writer, it presents an idealized image of how he would like to live. "I hope I can organize the various aspects of my life as well as the house does," he says of its clear separation of functions. Marcelle does, however, see analogies between his present self and his upstate New York retreat, nestled among trees on a 40-acre site. For example, his "overdeveloped intellect" is expressed through the reading room Simon Ungers made for him and his 10,000 books—a double-height space cantilevered 14 feet over both sides of the kitchen to, in Marcelle's words, "deliberately overwhelm the rest of the house." Ungers's translation of Marcelle's personal vision and residential program into a straight-forward plan is remarkable considering that architect and client didn't meet until after a preliminary design was done. "It *is* unusual," concedes Ungers of the chain of events, "but I met his mother and she described him pretty well."

At first glance the T-House looks more like a giant sculpture by Richard Serra than a place to live, yet it incorporates many homey ideals. Its monumentality and rigid adherence to a system of proportion also give an overall effect of permanence, stability, and reassurance—characteristics of more traditional images of home. Taking advantage of the site, Ungers incorporated the topography of a former sand excavation pit, stepping the volumes down the hillside to exploit distant views of the Berkshire Mountains.

The design's determined repetition and precision—all exposed vertical surfaces are punctured by rows of 8-foot-high by 2-foot-wide windows, which, on the interior, alternate with 8-foot-high and 2-foot-wide wood panels fastened at 2-foot intervals—served the architect in construction, a painstaking process in this case since the exterior shell was pre-assembled in six parts and transported by flatbed to the site (below), where it had to be fitted to concrete foundations. Final welding and grinding of the weathering steel plate was done on site, and there are no expansion joints to disrupt the overall monolithic effect. Unlike the seamless exterior, interior joints are revealed: mahogany panels are separated by 1/4 inch to show their frame, and cork is used below the baseboards to allow for expansion and emphasize the edges where walls meet floors.

Even though the T-House is barely visible from the road, Ungers had to obtain a variance in order to build up to its 42-foot height. The unusual design raised objections from the local zoning board, but after delay of almost a year, approval for the project was granted. "The house you build is like the clothes you wear," say Marcelle of the public design-review process. "Your decisions should be private, but they get judged in public." *Karen D. Stein*

The 1/4-inch-thick steel exterior shell was prefabricated in six parts and then transported to the site, where it was assembled on top of concrete foundations (photo below left). The steel's nickel and chromium finish has oxidized to a vibrant rust color.

The lower level of the house is 84 feet long from kitchen to bedroom (plans right and opposite). In the center of the 14-foot-wide loft-like space is a steel chimney (above). To accommodate the different expansion rates of steel and wood, interior walls comprise an independent structural frame. Two-foot-wide panels veneered with plantation-grown mahogany are fastened by black painted screws at two-foot intervals to a kiln-dried poplar frame. The bedroom has an Ungers-designed Murphy bed shown closed (top) and open (bottom).

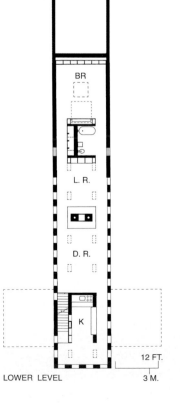

LOWER LEVEL

12 FT.

3 M.

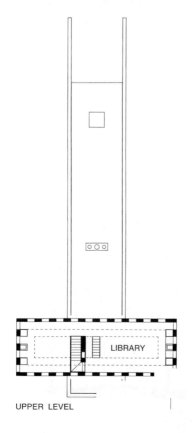

UPPER LEVEL

LIBRARY

Entry to the house (photo above) is between the living level below and double-height library above (plans left and opposite). The kitchen (top left) has stainless-steel shelves; the stainless-steel bathroom fixtures (bottom left) come from prison-supply manufacturers. Floors are made of teak salvaged from rivers in Burma.

The volume of the house is divided in half by a central wall (opposite) separating the two-story living room (bottom left) from the dining/kitchen area (top and middle left). The wall, however, is not perceived as a planar element.

Credits
Saito House
Houston, Texas
Owner: *Yoko Saito*
Architect: *Carlos Jimenez Architectural Design Studio— Carlos Jimenez, designer; Dominique Brousseau, Kendall Hamman, Eric Batte, project team*
Engineer: *Structural Consulting Company (structural)*

Castle Cloud

On a vast sweeping Pacific Coast site, Joan Hallberg gives fresh meaning to the notion that one's home is one's castle.

Private Residence
Stewart's Point, California
Joan Hallberg, Architect

erched high above the wild craggy Pacific Coast south of Sea Ranch, California, this expansive house is a tribute to an architect's commitment to her concept. What Joan Hallberg had in mind was a castle: a commanding structure filled with grand spaces, open and accessible, but enclosed and secure as well. She felt the idea suited the 220-acre site with its rugged outcroppings. And it most certainly fit her client. "He's very big," she says, referring to both his physical presence and outgoing nature.

"He wanted a series of pods," she recalls—stretched out parallel to the spectacular views, and isolated from each other to express different functions and allow house guests to escape the noise and clatter of up to 40 other visitors who might drop in on a typical weekend, or the 300 who might show up for special parties. But a series of discrete units would be lost against such a sweeping backdrop. "It was too overwhelming," Hallberg says of the site she and the client had agreed on after exploring many possibilities. To satisfy two concepts seemingly at odds, she looked at the fog that often hovers over the ocean in long horizontal bands of clouds. "Rock forms lay below the clouds. Some engaged them, and others popped through." This would be the way that 6,200 feet of living space, anchored solidly to the ground, would be united under one protective cover.

Hallberg has indeed produced a castle, very much of this time, but timeless nonetheless. Its spartan, straightforward detailing in all-natural materials, and intricacies of scale—ever changing with the vantage point of the viewer, from intimate to massive—all spell out her intentions. In some places, the viewer is able to reach up and touch the roof trusses that range from flexibly bolted steel for the floating roof, to rigidly welded steel, to heavy timber, depending on their lateral-bracing and loading functions. In other places, the trusses are 16 feet overhead. Hallberg tied steel-pipe supports for her floating-roof trusses through the wood structure, down to the top plate of the first floor. Open iron-grid catwalks slope between steel C-section stringers so that the visitor is at normal height to the railing at one end but well below it at the other. "You feel it's your scale changing," she notes of such design manipulations. "I did as much work on sections as plans," she explains of her working method. With the catwalks, Hallberg had her greatest opportunity to introduce a primeval effect: one is vulnerable to the natural forces of wind and waves—all modulated by open and closed sections of roof above.

Hallberg created these poetic effects with much problem-solving. First came the difficulty of meeting strict state energy-code requirements. Under this code, the warm East Bay area and Stewart's Point, located 130 miles to the north, were included in the same climatological zone. Requirements mainly intended to limit the cooling loads of the East Bay put restrictions on the glass-to-floor-area ratio—a particular problem for a site with great views—even though this location is naturally cool. She solved the problem using low-emissivity glass, which allowed her to increase the glass to 52 percent of the floor area.

Tying the building elements together structurally presented other difficulties, but was accomplished using enormous cross-braced drag-beam foundations. "It was the largest concrete pour on the coast at that time," she recalls. A builder framed the structure and closed it in, the trusses were fabricated under separate contract, and finally the owner took over as general contractor and employed numerous local craftspeople to finish the building partly as a gesture of good will to the community. At first she was dubious about his approach. "It was all very labor intensive," she recalls. "But the house came out beautifully," she admits. *Charles K. Hoyt*

© *Alan Wentraub photos*

Heavy winds, the weight of up to 300 guests, and brush fires were among the design problems. An extra-heavy structure and a galvanized-steel roof over rigid insulation were the solutions.

The only painted surfaces are the exterior steel. Inside, steel is exposed, protected by a light zinc-dip coating, which takes on a blue-gray color.

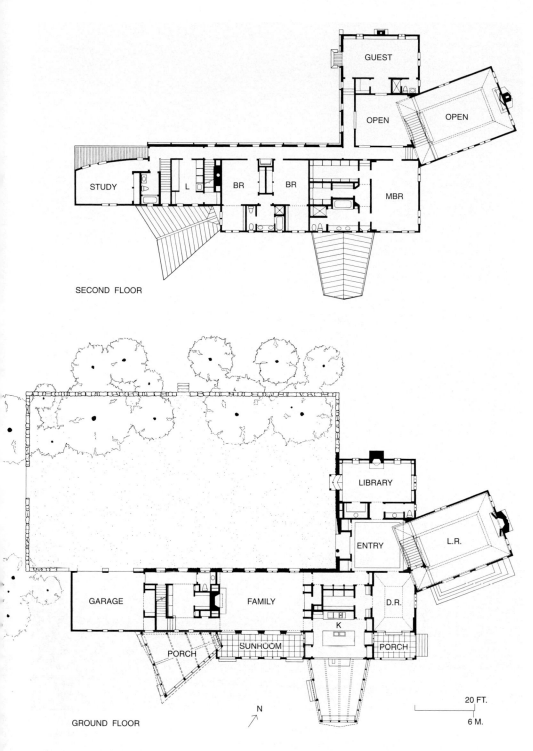

SECOND FLOOR

GUEST

OPEN

OPEN

STUDY

L

BR

BR

MBR

LIBRARY

ENTRY

L.R.

GARAGE

FAMILY

D.R.

PORCH

SUNROOM

K

PORCH

N

20 FT.

6 M.

GROUND FLOOR

By arranging the plan in an L shape, the architects created separate entertaining, family-living, and child zones, while maintaining comfortable adjacencies among them. Although the second-floor hallway is 85 feet long (plans above), staircases at both ends ease circulation up and down. Children's rooms are stacked above the family room and kitchen—the main gathering space—and the master-bedroom suite is clustered near the library and more formal living room. The paved courtyard framed by slate and cedar walls (opposite top) contrasts with the grassy hillside and its less formal white-painted wood face (opposite bottom).

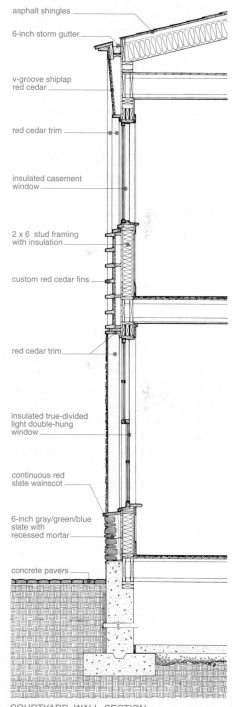

asphalt shingles

6-inch storm gutter

v-groove shiplap red cedar

red cedar trim

insulated casement window

2 x 6 stud framing with insulation

custom red cedar fins

red cedar trim

insulated true-divided light double-hung window

continuous red slate wainscot

6-inch gray/green/blue slate with recessed mortar

concrete pavers

COURTYARD WALL SECTION

Cover it up!

Metal retrofit can solve the problem. MBCI'S NuRoof™ can make it easy.

Manufacturer Sources

For your convenience in locating building materials and other products shown in this month's feature articles, RECORD has asked the architects to identify the products specified.

Pages 64-71
Private Residence
Carlos Zapata Design Studio, Architect
Structural stainless-steel columns: Advance Metal Fabricators. Green-tinted laminated glass: HGP Industries, Inc. Steel-framed windows, curtain wall, and Italian onyx glazing: A/P Glass and Window (custom). Stainless-steel beaded doors and tensioned-cable railings: Marine Design, Inc. Interior wood and sliding doors: Hollywood Woodworks, Inc. Locksets: Modric. Pivot hinges: Rixon. Lime-based sand and pigment paint: Cianfoni Art Restoration, Inc. Wall-wash and exterior lighting fixtures: Elliptipar. Pin spots: CSL Lighting Mfg., Inc.

Pages 72-75
Stringfellow Residence
Lubowicki/Lanier Architects
Metal roof: Flat-seamed lead-coated copper. Exterior siding, wood windows, interior doors, and woodwork: vertical-grain Douglas fir, fabricated by Alexander Construction. Clear exterior finish: Thompson Water Seal. Steel-frame windows and custom skylight: Torrance Steel Windows. Lever handles: Wagenfeld. Locksets: Modric. In-floor electric outlets: Hubbell. Floor grilles: Metalmorphosis (custom). Gray French-limestone flooring: EuroTile. Gypsum wet plaster: USG Corp., installed by Sy Feldman Plastering. Pin spot lights: CSL Lighting Mfg., Inc.

Pages 76-83
House on Turtle Creek
Antoine Predock, Architect
Cementitious stucco, cast-in-place concrete, and polished-concrete flooring: Texas Industries. Steel-frame windows and entrances: Hope's Architectural Products. Curved, tempered, and laminated glass: Tempglass, Inc. Division of Indal, Inc.; fabricated by Layne Glass. Roofing membrane: Soprema. Wood doors and custom cabinetry: Leinberger Construction. Paints and stains: Glidden Co. Hydraulic elevator: Dover. Recessed lighting: Edison Price, Inc. Cold-cathode lighting: Neotech. Steplights: Vega. Special fixtures: Fontana Arte.

Pages 84-89
Von Stein Residence
Fernau & Hartman Architects
Integral-color cement stucco: La Habra Stucco. Opaque stain on wood siding: Samuel Cabot. Aluminum-framed windows: Bonelli. Lever-handle locksets: Baldwin Hardware Mfg. Co. Hinges: McKinney. Paints: Fuller O'Brien. Stain on concrete: Conrad-Sovig. Exterior lighting: Appleton, McPhilben

Pages 90-95
T-House
Simon Ungers and Tom Kinslow, Architects
Weathering-steel structure and 1/4-in-thick cladding panels: Bethlehem Steel Co. Black-enameled steel windows and entrance system: Hope's Architectural Products, Inc. Solid-core wood doors and plantation-grown mahogany-veneer-plywood paneling: M.H. Judge & Co. Steel grating on stairs and library shelving: Irving, fabricated by Westside Ironworks. Bathroom sink and toilet: Bradley Corp. Bathtub: custom. Light fixtures: Metalux. Kitchen shelving: V.F. Connors. Kitchen faucets: Chicago Faucets.

Pages 96-99
Saito Residence
Carlos Jimenez Architectural Design Studio
Pine siding: Boise Cascade. Exterior and interior paints: Benjamin Moore & Co. Shingle roofing: Celotex Corp. Exterior spotlights: Hubbell, Inc. Double-glazed wood windows: Marvin Windows. Hollow-metal and wood-framed doors: Lonestar Wood Products. Door hardware: Stanley. Locksets: Schlage Lock Co. White-oak flooring: Ruth Jebelli Floors. Sisal carpeting: Bigelow. Recessed incandescent fixtures: Lightolier, Inc. Window blinds: Levolor Corp. Cooktop: Gaggenau. Ovens: General Electric.

Pages 100-105
Private Residence
Joan Hallberg, Architect
Structural roof trusses: Vulcraft Div. Nucor Corp. Sheet-metal roofing: Galvalume. Aluminum-framed windows: Milgard Mfg., Inc. Galvanized-steel gratings: Arrowhead Grating. Custom cabinetry: Gualala Joinery. Low-voltage lighting (dining room): Targetti.

Pages 106-111
Private Residence
Machado and Silvetti Associates, Inc., Architect
Exterior siding: Red Cedar with opaque white stain. Metal roof: standing-seam copper. Double-hung and casement windows: Pozzi Window Co. Stone infill and flooring: Vermont Slate. Recessed lighting: Prescolite. Cooktop: Thermador. Kitchen faucets: Chicago Faucet Co. Door hardware: Jado. Interior paints: Donald Kaufman Custom Paints.

1995

At 40 years old, RECORD HOUSES enters mid-life, an appropriate time to take stock. We've featured hundreds of houses over the years, and made, it seems, some indelible impressions in the minds of our readers. In fact, last month, of "the 10 contemporary houses that matter most to architects" listed in *The New York Times Magazine*, six had been first published in ARCHITECTURAL RECORD (five were covers). Hardly, we think, a coincidence. It's too early to predict the influence of this year's lineup of nine projects, which includes the work of acknowledged masters of residential design—Gwathmey Siegel & Associates (page 74), Franklin D. Israel Design Associates (page 82), and Turner Brooks (page 92)—as well as emerging voices—Frederick Phillips & Associates (page 68), Koning Eizenberg Architecture, (page 88), and Hariri & Hariri (page 96)—and newcomers—Dean/Wolf (page 62) and Judith Sheine (page 70). Of all the designers featured, it is perhaps Ettore Sottsass (page 80), the 77-year-old Milanese architect, industrial designer, and de facto poet, who best sums up the diverse impulses that not only drive architects to constantly reinvent the house (a type that most consumers still prefer in a conventional mode), but also the mission of RECORD HOUSES: "There are moments when you want to go to the piazza and shout, and other times when you need to be more quiet."
Karen D. Stein

Manufacturers' Sources listed on page 107

Hitting Bedrock

Dean/Wolf Architects solidly anchors this hilltop house to a granite formation, affording both woodland views and privacy.

Spiral House
North Castle, New York
Dean/Wolf Architects

o many potential buyers, this site seemed impossible. A house *and* its septic-drain fields could occupy only some 10 percent of the three-plus acres because the rest was designated as protected wetlands. That restriction confined the possible site for a building to just one location—on top of a solid-granite dome tight against the rear property line (site plan below). Worse still, the driveway would have to cross a stream—which meant special-permit requirements—and climb up a jumble of craggy ledges—which meant blasting. But a young professional couple with several active pre-adolescents and a love for nature, Andrew and Lisa Greenberg, were intrigued by the site's beauty, including, in addition to the stream and ledges, dense woods containing trees over a 100 years old. Before they made an offer, however, they did what too few clients do. They called in the architect.

As the undaunted team of Kathryn Dean and Charles Wolf walked the difficult terrain with the Greenbergs, they quickly saw that the assets outweighed the deficits. One asset was the granite dome, which forms the highest elevation and offers the best views. Another factor, the proximity to the northern boundary, was not all bad: Across the property line is a manicured golf course offering protection against incursion by future houses going up too close by. On the south side, however, where the stream comes closest to the building site, the owners can enjoy the view against a background of dense trees shielding the public road beyond.

On the spot, clients and architects decided to focus the primary view towards woods and stream, and to turn a relatively blind entry side (opposite and previous pages) toward the golf course. Soon after, the Greenbergs approved Dean and Wolf's basic parti: an organizing spine for the spaces within and without, using angled walls on the entry side to form an upward-reaching spiral. The incline of the driveway, where it ends at a U-turn, carries through in the angle of flanking concrete screen walls (top right), which gradually rise from the ground to meet the house. There, the ascent continues along the top of a cedar-clad screen wall above the first floor (previous pages), then under the second-floor windows (left), where it terminates in a tall stone-faced fin wall. The building plan widens in tandem with the spiral's height (overleaf) so that the spaces inside flow horizontally, giving a forced-perspective view from the entrance door. They also flow vertically toward the sky through light wells enclosed with polished plaster walls that pass through the second floor, emphasizing the focus above.

Although the design went quickly, the following stages did not. Approvals by various authorities to cross wetlands and alter site contours took a year. Sitework called for highway-construction blast-borer equipment to place some 1,000 pounds of dynamite as the machines climbed ledges on heavy tracked rollers to build the driveway and ultimately to create a level area on the granite dome for a building site. (Some of the stone was salvaged for exterior facing, but plans to surface all the exterior as well as the living-room floor and fireplace with stone had to be abandoned because the cost of setting it was too high.) One bonus was that concrete first-floor walls could be poured directly on the newly created granite surface. The owner took responsibility for subcontracting site preparation and foundations, a process that Wolf says worked well. But he adds: "There has to be a clear understanding of responsibilities." (While he declines to discuss the cost of this 6,100-square-foot house, he cites the case of another client who handled all subcontracting, saving 20 percent of estimated costs.) After the concrete, came a steel-frame structure for the second floor and, finally, finishes, including windows framed in marine-grade teak outside and ash within. *Charles K. Hoyt*

The granite outcropping (opposite) is the remaining portion of the original terrain before it was leveled and became a construction site. It forms a focus around which the house now turns.

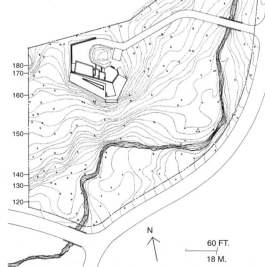

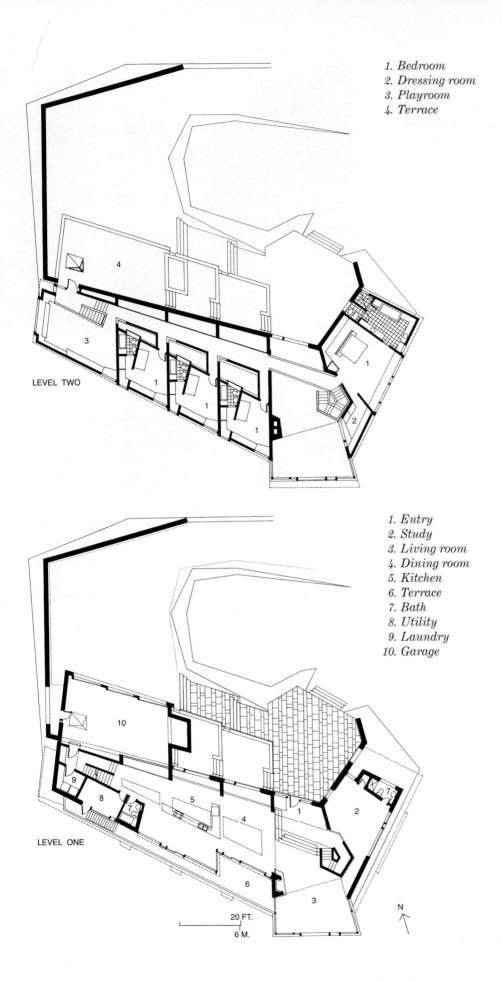

1. Bedroom
2. Dressing room
3. Playroom
4. Terrace

LEVEL TWO

1. Entry
2. Study
3. Living room
4. Dining room
5. Kitchen
6. Terrace
7. Bath
8. Utility
9. Laundry
10. Garage

LEVEL ONE

20 FT.

6 M.

N

"There isn't a right angle in the place," says Charles Wolf in only a slight exaggeration. Considering the angled walls and roofs that slope in two directions—laterally for drainage and longitudinally to express the design parti—the joint connections in the house's concrete-and-steel construction had to be flexible.

A forced perspective created by converging walls can be seen in the upstairs hall (opposite left). Here, the walls around skylit wells to the floor below (opposite) also slope. Small glazed windows in these walls provide acoustic privacy to the living area when the owners' children make noise.

All interior trim is ash and the wood floors are white oak stained with a water-based finish that prevents yellowing in the abundant sunlight.

The end of the living room (opposite) is cantilevered 14 feet out from a cliff to bring stream views closer. Concrete transverse fin walls along the north wall (plan) provide lateral structural support and are hidden from view outside by cedar screen walls that carry the slope of the upward-spiral parti .

Credits
Spiral House
North Castle, New York
Owners: *Dr. Andrew and Lisa Goldberg*
Architect: *Dean/Wolf Architects—Kathryn Dean, Charles Wolf, partners-in-charge*
Engineer: *Anchor Consulting (structural)—Evan Akselrad, partner-in-charge*
Consultant: *Reginald Hough (concrete)*
General Contractor: *Einar Moi*

Chicago Shotgun

The comparatively spacious 40-foot-wide double lot architect Frederick Phillips had as a starting point for a doctor's residence presented a challenge: how to preserve the scale and rhythm of a neighborhood of narrow houses built on 20-foot-wide lots. "The temptation would be to cover the whole lot with one structure that would present a cube-shaped barrier to the street," says Phillips. Instead, he designed a narrow ground- and split-face concrete block shotgun-like house for the west half of the lot. With the exception of a garage at the rear of the site, and the structural-steel framed porch and bedroom tower, he left the east half of the lot open for use as a garden.

The steel porch and bedroom structure was carefully detailed. "I had made several trips to South Carolina, and had become familiar with some masonry houses, with post-and-beam porches on the sides to catch the prevailing breezes. Visually, we wanted the porch to feel light; to be something that says the light structure is there to be a filter for breezes."

Another challenge for Phillips in this transitional neighborhood, where gangs are active, was meeting his client's need for security and secure access for patients. Three parking spaces were provided inside the rear garage, so that patients can park inside the building, and few windows were provided on the first floor. Security gates were installed at some vulnerable entry points on the second floor. *Charles Linn*

Credits
Private Residence
Chicago, Illinois
Architect: *Frederick Phillips & Associates—Frederick Phillips, design principal; Ronald Piekarz, project architect; Brian Buczkowski, production architect*
Engineer: *Stearn Joglekar*
General Contractor: *Frederick Phillips & Associates*

Private Residence
Frederick Phillips & Associates,
Architect
Chicago, Illinois

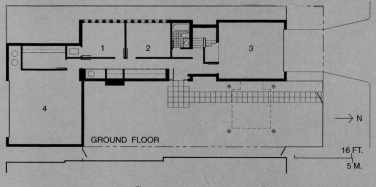

GROUND FLOOR

→ N

16 FT.
5 M.

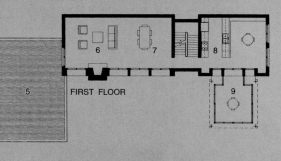

FIRST FLOOR

SECOND FLOOR

1. *Storage*
2. *Office*
3. *Garage*
4. *Garage*
5. *Deck*
6. *Living room*
7. *Dining room*
8. *Kitchen*
9. *Porch*
10. *Master bedroom*
11. *Bedroom*
12. *Bedroom*

Desert Outcropping

Sarli Residence
Juniper Hills, California
Judith Sheine, Architect

Only an hour and a half northeast of Los Angeles, in the foothills of the San Gabriel Mountains and on the way to the Mojave Desert, lies Juniper Hills, a world apart. Here, at an elevation of 4,200 feet, John Sarli, a mathematician and avid outdoorsman, purchased five acres of rolling terrain to satisfy both vocation and avocation—contemplation and intense athletic activity. He asked Judith Sheine, a friend from college, an architect and currently a professor at UCLA and Cal Poly, Pomona, to build him, in his words, "a crystal-like structure, a gem in the desert."

Sheine, a self-proclaimed disciple of Rudolph Schindler (and co-editor of a recent book on Schindler's work and writings, published by Academy Editions) has absorbed many lessons from the master—most notably, faith in a flexible four-foot module that could be sub-divided or multiplied and, because of Schindler's training as an engineer, his vision of himself as an "artist-builder," according to Sheine. These traits are in evidence in her first completed house.

The architect placed the structure on an existing narrow promontory near the middle of the site, flanked by steep drop-offs ideal for drainage. Set at 45 degrees from due north, the profile of the curved metal roof split into two uneven pieces gently echoes rolling hills that loom in the distance, while giving the effect of an alien vessel. Says Sheine of the striking form and choice of materials: "It's like a *Barbarella* spaceship. Hard on the outside and soft on the inside." Indeed, the steel roof decking set atop 16-inch-thick load-bearing perimeter walls (4 inches of rigid insulation sandwiched between an 8-inch-wide concrete block and 4-inch-wide exterior face block) contrasts with the soft yellow sheen of the birch-veneer plywood lining that rises from 8 feet 8 inches above the block to the 16 foot 8-inch centerline of the curved main vault (following pages).

Like Schindler, Sheine, a former student of mathematics, based the proportions of the main spaces on a four-foot module: the 16-foot-wide interior space is divided into three sections: a 12-foot-long bedroom; a 20-foot-long kitchen and bathroom block organized around a three-sided courtyard; and a 28-foot-long living/dining room. Lofts suspended from the roof decking by 1/4-inch steel cables provide additional sleeping/reading space at both ends of the house. Steel beams are highlighted by a red primer coat that acts as a paint color (similar to San Francisco's Golden Gate Bridge), reinforcing the reddish hue of custom-designed Douglas fir window frames.

Located in an active earthquake zone, the structure withstood the strong vertical shear of the 1994 Northridge earthquake. The materials, however, are not immune to the elements. Harsh sunlight rapidly discolors window frames and the metal roofing expands and contracts depending on daylight, emitting muffled expansion creaks as the sun emerges in the morning. Says Sarli of his new home: "It's an alarm clock." *Karen D. Stein*

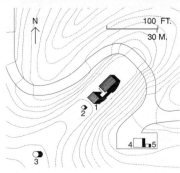

The house sits on a plateau atop the hilly five-acre site; its length runs northeast to southwest. Future plans include a terraced path between house and garage.

1. House
2. Pump house
3. Water tank
4. Garage
5. Well house

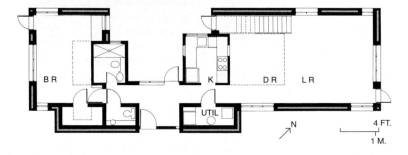

Steel decking on the ceiling is
18-gauge and 4 1/2-inches deep,
allowing room to recess sprin-
klers. On the bottom of the loft
it's 16-gauge and 3-inches deep.
The dining room wall is clad in
corrugated steel with a subtle
leaf-like pattern from the finishing process. Above the 8-foot
8-inch-high concrete block walls,
birch veneer plywood panels are
screwed to metal studs.

Credits
Sarli Residence
Juniper Hills, California
Owner: *John Sarli*
Architect: *Judith Sheine,*
Architect
Engineers: *Gerald Sheine and*
Nancy Hamilton
General Contractor: *Joseph T.*
Setter

1. *18-gauge*
   structural steel
   decking
2. *1/2-inch plywood*
3. *20-gauge*
   corrugated steel
   roofing
4. *Torch-applied*
   roofing
5. *Rigid insulation*
6. *Gutter formed*
   from steel
7. *Concrete block*
8. *Rigid insulation*

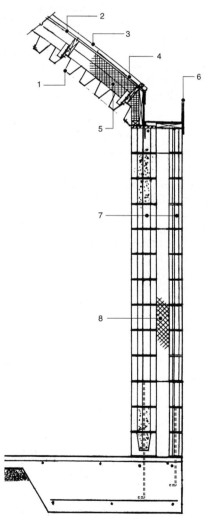

PERIMETER WALL SECTION

BR   K   DR   LR

UTIL

N   4 FT.
           1 M.

Living With Art

On a hill overlooking Lake Zurich, this large house mimics a small village.

Speaking Softly

Having contributed some of the more colorful and energetic designs of the roaring 80s—from his Memphis furniture to his showrooms for Esprit—Ettore Sottsass is in a different mood these days. "There are moments when you want to go to the piazza and shout," explains the Milan-based designer, "and other times when you need to be more quiet." While designing the Casa Cei, a 4,800-square-foot house for a family of four in Tuscany, Sottsass felt the pull of ancient traditions and let them help shape the building.

As a result, Casa Cei is an exercise in simple geometry: a cubic form clad in white Istrian stone, topped with a red metal roof, and surrounded by an unpretentious garden. "Tuscan architecture is very compact, dignified, symmetrical," says Sottsass. "Houses here have a sense of mystery and silence, like a de Chirico painting." Any trace of menace at Casa Cei, though, is dispelled by the light touch of Sottsass and his associates Marco Zanini and Mike Ryan in the colorful frames surrounding windows and a balcony. "The windows are toys glued onto the Classical white box," explains Sottsass.

Designed for a middle-class family with traditional Italian ways

© *Santi Caleca photos*

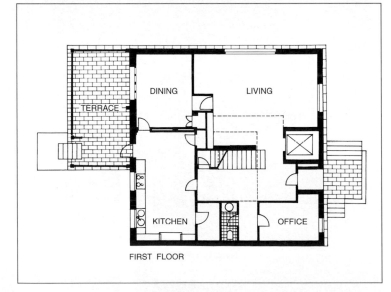

FIRST FLOOR

TERRACE · DINING · LIVING · KITCHEN · OFFICE

SECOND FLOOR

BEDROOM · BEDROOM · BEDROOM

(everyone gathers for lunch at home every day, for example), the house has a simple concrete frame with brick infill and a metal-truss roof that seems to float above stone-clad walls. Whereas the exterior emphasizes the house's solidity, the interiors are surprisingly light, thanks to a central atrium that brings sunlight in from above. The same third-story windows that let in all that light also draw hot air out of the house when they are opened during warm months. On the ground floor, a large Tuscan-style kitchen allows the entire family to gather and a two-story-high living room provides an elegant space for socializing. The second floor is mostly bedrooms, while the third floor has a guest room and a wrap-around terrace offering views of the ancient Tuscan hills. *Clifford A. Pearson*

Credits
Casa Cei
Tuscany, Italy
Architect: *Sottsass Associati—Ettore Sottsass, Marco Zanini, Mike Ryan, design team*
Associate Architect: *Studio Maestrelli*
General Contractor: *COE*

Casa Cei
Tuscany, Italy
Sottsass Associati, Architect
Studio Maestrelli, Associate
Architect

THIRD FLOOR   N   16 FT.

GUEST

TERRACE

5 M.

EAST - WEST SECTION

10 FT.

3 M.

Blending suburban building types, the Drager house is a split-level that rises up a steep hill, soon to be filled with larger houses. The gridded street-front facade melds several traditions, including Rudolf Schindler, a favorite source for Israel, and the bungalows with articulated wood structures and strong roof profiles common to the neighborhood.

At the center of the structure is the point of entry, the "great hall," around which the main public rooms are arranged. The living room fills the width of the house and borrows light from both sides.

N

24 FT.
7 M.

LOWER LEVEL

SECOND LEVEL

ENTRY LEVEL

UPPER LEVEL

1. Garage
2. Storage
3. Family room
4. Guest room
5. Living room
6. Kitchen
7. Dining room
8. Office
9. Master bedroom
10. Bedroom

SECTION LOOKING EAST

SECTION LOOKING WEST

Family Matters

31st Street House
Santa Monica, California
Koning Eizenberg Architecture,
Architects

Unlike neighbors in more affluent sections of town, the clients for this project (a couple with two children) wanted changes to their 1930s Santa Monica cottage to be virtually invisible from the street (top right). For architects Hank Koning and Julie Eizenberg, known for both commercial and residential work [RECORD, Mid-April 1988, pages 90-95], the compact 40-foot by 150-foot site presented little obvious room to maneuver; nonetheless, they managed to assert their presence. Says Eizenberg of their small, yet forceful addition: "We were well behaved."

Local zoning ordinances prohibited adding more than 50 percent of the existing square footage of 1,300 unless, among other things, garage space was doubled. Koning, Eizenberg, and project architect Tim Andreas were able to reorganize an inefficient floor plan and pack in 650 square feet more, mostly in the second floor of a chunky 21-foot-high tower that does not exceed the area's height limit of 28 feet (bottom right and opposite). The tower also provides sheltered outdoor dining in the courtyard. For design clues, the architects looked to Irving Gill, whose stucco-covered cubic forms and signature strips of rectangular windows reappear here.

While a thickened chimney in the front acts as a privacy screen along the street, new windows pushed to the perimeter and around the front corners generously admit light and give the impression of a floating roof. The architects removed an interior dropped ceiling, lining the underside of the newly exposed gable with wood and reinforcing the structure with tie rods, which, when painted the same butter color as the walls, almost disappear. They smoothed out the odd volumetric ins and outs of the south wall by moving the kitchen and a cramped, formal dining room out into the open and reconfiguring leftover space into a powder room and maid's room. Unlike Gill's houses, which are characterized by compact, densely interwoven rooms, this interior now has the feel of a sprawling loft, borrowing light and space from adjacent areas. In the sitting room, oversized Douglas fir-framed sliding doors overlook a paved courtyard that is shielded from the house next door by a concrete block wall, extending the room into the garden. It's Koning and Eizenberg's blurring of the lines between inside and outside that gives new vigor to the original interior, without turning the house into a public spectacle.
Karen D. Stein

To retain a modest street-front facade, the architects did minimum renovation to the house front (top right), saving their architectural expression for a backyard master-bedroom tower, which peeks out over the main volume (bottom right). Stucco arches flare out 18-inches—a massive base for a glass-rimmed suite (opposite).

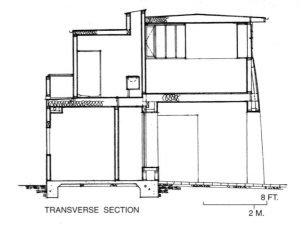

TRANSVERSE SECTION

8 FT.

2 M.

The architects opened up a warren of enclosed rooms to create a loft-like series of linked areas that borrow space and light from one another. The former kitchen and dining area were gutted and are now a powder room and maid's quarters with a separate entrance from the side courtyard (plan below). The new kitchen is a wide corridor, connecting living/dining with a sitting room. A tower covers an outdoor eating area (photos left) and houses the master bedroom. Bands of green rectangular windows are studied reminders of Irving Gill (opposite).

Credits
31st Street House
Santa Monica, California
Owners: *Joanne and Philippe Valli-Marill*
Architect: *Koning Eizenberg Architecture—Hank Koning, Julie Eizenberg, principals-in-charge; Tim Andreas, project architect; Brian Lane, team*
Engineer: *Ross Downey & Associates*
General Contractor: *Charles Kuipers Design*

MBR

SECOND FLOOR

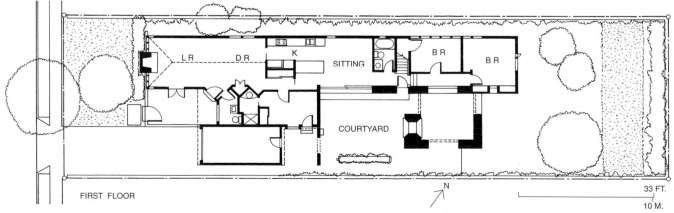

LR   DR   K   SITTING   BR   BR

COURTYARD

FIRST FLOOR

N

33 FT.
10 M.

Lombard/Miller House
Westby, Wisconsin
Brooks & Carey, Architect

© Cervin Robinson photos

Snazzy House

During two decades of practicing in northern Vermont, T[...] has designed a series of small buildings of special forma[...] originality, using wood-frame construction and vernacul[...] The owners of this latest house, artists Sharon Lombar[...] Miller, had moved from Cincinnati to rural Wisconsin, s[...] quil place in which to live, work, and raise their daughte[...] wanted what Lombard calls "an ostentatious money-sta[...] they wanted, instead, a house that would comfortably fit[...] regional landscape of fields and hills and the local societ[...] farms and small towns.

The couple learned of Brooks's houses in magazine artic[...] their verve and inventiveness. Of particular interest was[...] York City in which they noticed one of Brooks's toy-like[...] Creatures." Though a distant cousin of that work, the L[...] Miller house still has distinct features that relate to it, in[...] gutsy, exposed wood truss that helps define dining and li[...] a splayed stair that narrows as it ascends; a double-hung[...] installed diagonally; and interior windows of various size[...] echoing the architect's earlier work is the house's arrang[...]

Lombard is a performance artist, and her parents, who live nearby, are puppeteers. Thus the house incorporates elements that encourage small-scale theatrical performances: a platform in the living room, which Brooks calls a "makeshift stage," and the exterior stairs that cascade down from the kitchen porch create impromptu bleachers. Other elements with stage presence include a balcony and several interior windows. Recently, a bedroom window played a major role in a children's party, serving as the launch point for "flying ants," made of candy bars lowered to excited guests below. The living/dining/kitchen space is finished in a lively combination of materials: walls are fir plywood, painted wood wainscoting, and drywall; the floors are maple. The dining table and chairs were designed by Brooks.

Credits

Lombard/Miller House
Westby, Wisconsin
Architect: Brooks & Carey—
Turner Brooks, principal;
Dennis Willmott, Thomas
Warner, associates
Consultants: Arthur Choo
(structural); John Bates
(lighting)
General Contractor:
Daniel Arnold

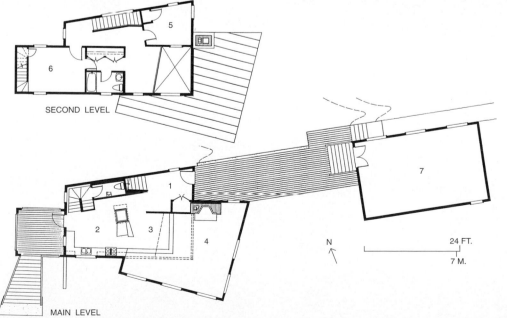

SECOND LEVEL

MAIN LEVEL

1. Entry
2. Kitchen
3. Dining room
4. Living room
5. Bedroom
6. Master bedroom
7. Studio

N

24 FT.

7 M.

Canadian Au Pair

Barry's Bay Cottage
Ontario, Canada
Hariri & Hariri, Architect

queezed between an existing A-frame cottage that the clients wanted to keep for sentimental reasons and a grove of tall birch trees, the 2,500-square-foot addition designed by Gisue and Mojgan Hariri is a Modernist long-house shaped by the boats, trees, and vistas found in this rustic part of Ontario near Barry's Bay. A summer home for a Virginia couple and their four grown children, it is a place where the horizontal thrust of the nearby lake and the vertical pull of the slender birches are perfectly balanced. It is also a place where the tightly spaced structures create an almost palpable sense of compression, while their shared deck spreads out toward expansive views.

As in their Gorman Residence in Connecticut [RECORD, April 1993, pages 76-83], the Hariri sisters faced the challenge of adding on to an undistinguished, pitched-roof house. Steeped in the Corbusian Modernism taught at Cornell in the 1970s, the Hariris might have been expected to emphasize the contrasts between old and new, vernacular and Modern. But in neither project did the architects take such a contrasting approach. In the Gorman Residence, they penetrated the old house with a new glass-and-steel bridge that, literally and figuratively, ties the entire composition together. In Ontario, they pushed the new structure to within three feet of the old, creating a long narrow alley that links two buildings and two design vocabularies together. "In Connecticut, we overlapped and penetrated spaces, while here we dealt with the separation of spaces and volumes," says Gisue Hariri.

Although distinct structures, the two components of the Barry's Bay project work as a single house with one kitchen, dining room, living area, and deck. Responding to questions from the local zoning board, the architects showed that a house isn't defined by one roof. By creating two components, the Hariris allowed the clients' children to entertain in the old house without disturbing their parents in the addition. At the same time, shared deck areas accommodate outdoor dining and relaxing. And the placement of two buildings so close together creates a tension that is released in dramatic fashion as the rear deck spreads out in a graceful curve to embrace both structures.

Although the addition echoes the pitched roof and wood siding of the old cottage, its clearly expressed structure and clean lines proclaim its Modernist lineage. Built on wood beams resting on concrete piers, the new structure's frame construction allowed the east facade to be punctured with long slot windows that the architects say recall the horizontal lines on birch bark. Metal pipe railings, along with wood decking and long cedar wall planks, hint at the nautical theme inspired by the lake and the boat-storage room that occupies a large part of the house's lower level.

Maintaining a simple palette of materials, the interiors are flowing spaces that overlook the lake without sacrificing a sense of enclosure. Indeed, it is this balancing of opposites that is becoming a hallmark of the Hariris' work to date. *Clifford A. Pearson*

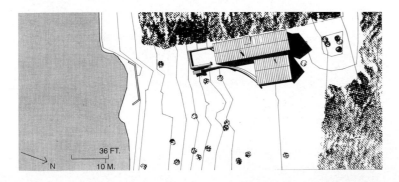

36 FT.
N   10 M.

Treating the existing prefabricated A-frame cottage as a given, the Hariris repaired its old foundations and stripped it of its fake shutters and pink paint. The new 100-foot-long addition is a frame structure built on wood beams resting on concrete piers (drawings right). A small pavilion topped with a wave-like roof projects beyond the house and encloses an outdoor shower (opposite, top). Slot windows intended to evoke the horizontal markings on birch bark cut into the east facade (opposite, middle) and act as light sources at night when the house is lit up and people are outside on the deck.

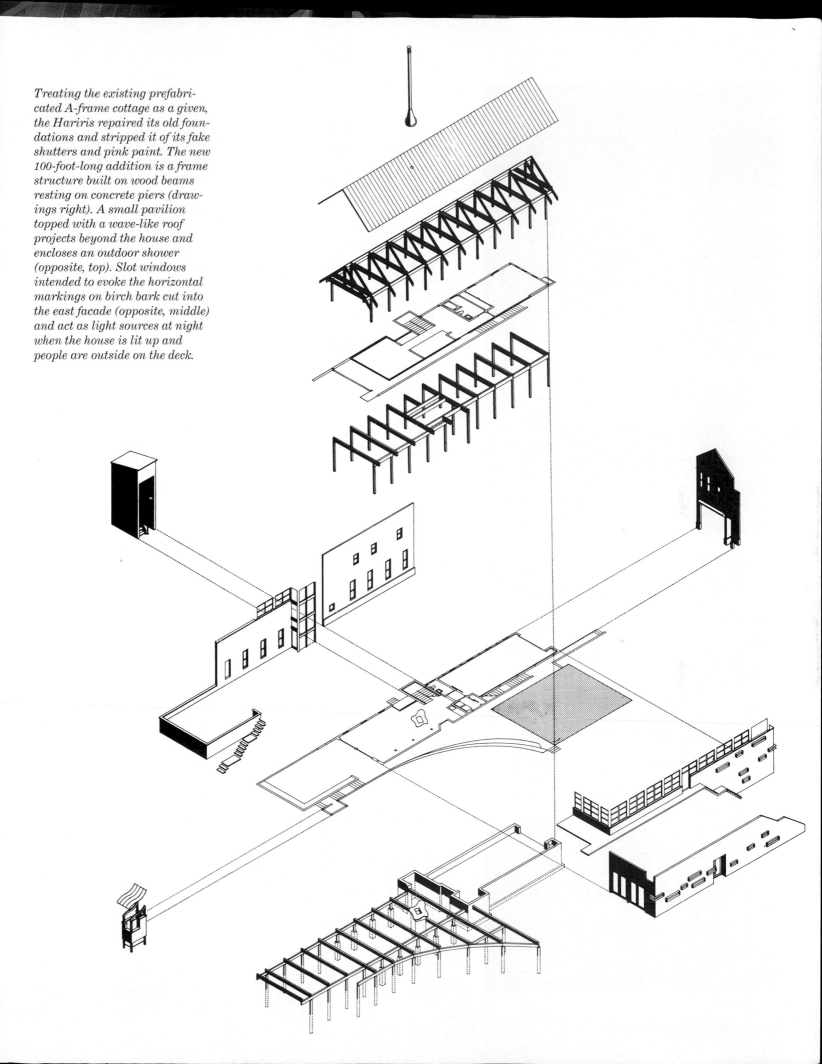

RECORD INTERIORS 1995

The editors of ARCHITECTURAL RECORD announce the 26th annual RECORD INTERIORS awards program. This program is open to any registered architect; work previously published in other national design magazines is disqualified. Of particular interest are projects that incorporate innovative programs, building technologies, and use of materials. There is an entry fee of $15 per submission; please make checks payable to ARCHITECTURAL RECORD. Submissions must also include plan(s), photographs (transparencies, slides, or prints), and a brief project description bound firmly in an 8-1/2- by 11-in. folder—and be postmarked no later than April 30, 1995. Winning entries will be featured in the 1995 RECORD INTERIORS. Other submissions will either be returned or scheduled for a future issue. If you would like your entry returned, please include a self-addressed envelope with appropriate postage.

Submissions should be mailed to:
Karen D. Stein
RECORD INTERIORS
ARCHITECTURAL RECORD
1221 Avenue of the Americas
New York, New York 10020

Manufacturer Sources

For your convenience in locating building materials and other products shown in this month's feature articles, RECORD has asked the architects to identify the products specified.

Pages 62-67
Spiral House
Dean/Wolf Architects
Siding: Clear-finished Western Red Cedar, Mary's River, Ore. Architectural concrete: Roger & Sons. Ash- and teak-framed windows and doors: Duratherm Window Corp. Brushed stainless-steel locksets: Omnia. EPDM roofing: Carlisle SynTec System. Lead-coated copper roof edge: fabricated by Rich Donsavage. Pavers: New York State Bluestone. Courtyard wall: granite from site, fabricated by Gary Bottino, Stone Mason. Skylights: Wasco. Exterior lighting: BEGA. Recessed downlights: Lightolier, Inc. Decorative fixtures: Akari; Artemide, Inc. Wood-floor finish: Miaco (oil-based polyurethane). Switch plates: Leviton (Decora). Paints: Benjamin Moore & Co. Carpet: Karastan. Railings: Patsy Ironworks. Low-voltage lighting: Tech Lighting. Kitchen floor: Tile Gallery, with tummeled limestone inset, Petrillo Stone.

Pages 68-69
Private Residence
Frederick Phillips & Associates, Architect
Aluminum-framed windows, doors: Acorn Window Systems. Locksets: Schlage Lock Co. Fence: custom, fabricated by Bayers Blacksmith. Paint on metal surfaces: Galvacon. Elastomeric roofing: U.S. Intec/Brai, Inc. Garage door: custom by architects, fabricated by Kelly Woodworks. Paints: Benjamin Moore & Co. Laminate countertops: Formica. Canvas roller shades: Glover Shade.

Pages 70-73
Sarli Residence
Judith Sheine, Architect
Metal roof decking: N.A.T. Industries. Glass and wood exterior doors: Douglas fir, custom. Locksets: Schlage Lock Co. Satin finish on birch-veneer plywood: Varathane. Windows: custom, fabricated by Chris Dangermond Woodworking. Aluminum pendant: Modernica.

Pages 82-87
Drager Residence
Franklin D. Israel Design Associates, Architect
Copper shingles: Durasystems. Garage door: Amarr. Entrances, wood windows, and cedar siding: custom by architects, fabricated by Fourth Street Woodworking+Roderick Smith. Window fittings: Truth Hardware. Locksets: Schlage Lock Co.; Adams Rite Co. Integral-color stucco and plaster: Beaton Plaster. Firebox: Superior Fireplace. Hearth: Purple slate. Paints: Benjamin Moore & Co.; Kelly Moore. Pin spots and recessed downlights: Capri. Drawer pulls: Hefele; Details. Chaise: Donghia. Architectural-metal railings: fabricated by Railmakers.

Pages 88-91
31st Street House
Koning Eizenberg Architecture, Architect
Paint on exterior stucco, interior paint: Dunn Edwards. Custom wood windows, sliders and garage doors: Charles Kuipers Design, Inc. Door knobs: Schlage Lock Co. Window shades: Advanced Floor & Window. Cementitious countertop: Syndecrete. Tile: Buchtal. Stove: Viking.

Pages 92-95
Lombard/Miller House
Brooks & Carey, Architect
Solid-white and red stains on red-cedar board and batten siding: Cabot's (OVT). Yellow paints: Benjamin Moore & Co. Double-hung and awning windows: Marvin Windows & Doors. Doors: Brosco. Finish on interior floors and paneling: Watco. Furniture: custom by architect, fabricated by Mike Burgess. Furniture stain: Mohawk. Locksets: Stanley. "Vapor proof" lights: Stonco. Kitchen sink: American-Standard. Exterior lighting: Killark.

Pages 96-101
Barry's Bay Cottage
Hariri and Hariri, Architect
Red Cedar tongue-and-groove siding: MacMillan Bloedel. Weathering stain: Thompson's Water Seal. Corrugated sheet metal: VicWest Steel. Windows: Donat Flamand, Inc. French-style doors: Pella Windows & Doors. Interior doors: Premdoor, Inc. Locksets: Weiser. Paints: Pittsburgh Paints. Tile floor: Olympia Tile. Upholstery fabric: Shyam Ahuja. Stainless-steel fireplace: custom by architect, fabricated by Zuracon Inc. Structural connections: Teco. Wall-mounted fixtures: Hubbell.